Dealing with Bullying in Schools

Professor Astrid Mona O'Moore is Head of the Department of Education and a Fellow of Trinity College Dublin, where she is the co-ordinator of the Anti-Bullying Research and Resource Centre. Her extensive training and research work in both schools and workplace bullying have won her international recognition.

Stephen James Minton is a researcher at the Anti-Bullying Research and Resource Centre, Trinity College Dublin, and is the Director of Training of the current Nationwide Intervention Programme against Bullying Behaviour in Irish Schools. He is a regular provider of training and presentations to various groups within school communities.

Dealing with Bullying in Schools

A Training Manual for Teachers, Parents and Other Professionals

Mona O'Moore

and

Stephen James Minton

Paul Chapman Publishing

London · Thousand Oaks · New Delhi

Paul Chapman Publishing
A SAGE Publications Company
1 Oliver's Yard
55 City Road
London EC1Y 1SP

SAGE Publications Inc
2455 Teller Road
Thousand Oaks, California 91320

SAGE Publications India Pvt Ltd
B-42 Panchsheel Enclave
Post Box 4109
New Delhi 110 017

Library of Congress Control Number 2003115418

A catalogue record for this book is available from the British Library

ISBN 1-4129-0280-0
ISBN 1-4129-0281-9 (pbk)

Typeset by Pantek Arts Ltd, Maidstone, Kent
Printed in Great Britain by Cromwell Press, Trowbridge.

Contents

Acknowledgements

The authors would like to acknowledge the support and continued good work of our colleagues at the Anti-Bullying Research and Resource Centre, Trinity College Dublin: Lian McGuire, Murray Smith, Dennis Blair, Karen Cahill, Anne Frey, Stephanie Loughman and Jean Lynch.

Mona O'Moore would like to thank in particular the Calouste Gulbenkian Foundation. It was their initial generous financial support together with that of the Department of Education and Science (Ireland) and the Arts and Social Science Benefaction Fund (Trinity College Dublin) which made it possible to conduct the nationwide study of bullying behaviour in Ireland and subsequently to pilot a national anti-bullying programme in Donegal. Both these studies have pointed to the need for this more practical comprehensive guidebook. This is not to take away from the depth of understanding that has been reached as a result of the many individuals, both adults and children, who through their courage and convictions have shared their experiences of victimization and bullying with me and the members of the Anti-Bullying Research and Resource Centre at Trinity College. I am also indebted to my husband Rory, and sons Garret, Olaf and Runar who have also contributed to shaping my understanding of bullying behaviour in both schools and workplaces by discussing their own observations and experiences.

Following the initial support of the above funding bodies, the authors would also like to thank the Irish Research Council for the Humanities and Social Sciences (IRCHSS) for their help to undertake on a national scale an anti-bullying programme in schools in Ireland. It is their generous support that has enabled the authors to develop this book which hopefully will contribute worldwide to a much needed reduction of bullying in school communities.

Stephen James Minton would also like to thank the following family members for their help and support over the years: my wife, Patricia Minton; my mother, Rosemary Elizabeth Fox; and also, for being a constant source of inspiration and joy, my baby daughter, Anna Rebecca Minton. On a professional level, my former project manager on the 'Pathways Through Education' project at the Dublin Institute of Technology, Dr Tommy Cooke, and the principals of the schools involved in that project – Michael Blanchfield and Sr Frances Murphy – deserve a special mention; all three, as well as Peter McCarney, were extremely helpful and encouraging during the years that I spent working on that project. I would also like to express my sincere appreciation to my former supervisor, Maureen Carmody, and to my friend Dr Lennart Karlsson.

Chapter 1

The problem of bullying

It is an odd thing that nearly everybody thinks that he or she knows what bullying is. For those of us who are now old enough to be parents, we might reflect upon what we were told about bullying when we were children. It is quite likely that the messages we received then would have been rather mixed; whilst no responsible person in recent times would support violence and abuse in wider society, a strange and illogical exception was sometimes made in the case of school bullying behaviour. Hence, it is quite possible that we grew up with a set of myths around bullying:

'It's part of life'.

'Boys will be boys – they'll blow off steam from time to time'.

'It happens in all schools, so it's nothing to worry about'.

'Sticks and stones may break your bones, but words will never harm you'.

'It never did me any harm'.

'It'll toughen you up/let you know what life's about', and so on.

Our answer to all of the above statements is a simple one: 'Nonsense. Absolute rubbish.' We feel confident in giving this response, because each of these 'myths' is simply that – a *myth*. Myths are ways in which people try to explain away, or make themselves feel better about matters that they have not properly investigated. But if we do try to look more deeply, we can find truths, rather than mere myths. For example, bullying does not have to be part of life. Bullying is not an instance of 'blowing off steam'. Bullying may occur in many schools, but it should be worried about, and should never be accepted. Words do cause harm, and bullying is always harmful. Being bullied never did anybody any favours – all it does is to destroy a person's confidence and self-esteem, and to cause physical, emotional and psychological damage of the potentially most serious and long-lasting kind.

As a society, our path to discovering the falsehood of these myths – and discovering what is quite self-evidently true – has been a surprisingly long one. Over the last twenty to thirty years, we have accrued (largely through educational and psychological research) a gradually clearer picture of the frequency and typology of bullying behaviour in schools, particularly in certain countries in Europe and in Australia. For example, a nationwide survey of bullying behaviour in Norway in autumn 1983 showed that 15 per cent of 7–16-year-old students were involved in bullying behaviour, 9 per cent as victims and 7 per cent as perpetrators. Of these, 1.6 per cent were involved as both.[1] A similar nationwide study in the Republic of Ireland showed that 31.3 per cent of primary-level students, and 15.6 per cent of post-primary students reported having been bullied within the last school term.[2] A regional survey in the United Kingdom showed that 27 per cent of primary pupils in sample of schools in Sheffield, South Yorkshire, in 1990, had been bullied 'sometimes' or more frequently, with 10 per cent of these having been bullied at least once per week. For their secondary school contemporaries, these figures were 10 per cent and 4 per cent respectively.[3] A survey undertaken in Scotland the year before had found that 6 per cent of 12–16-year-old students reported that they had been bullied, and 4 per cent said that they had been involved in bullying others.[4] Finally, in Australia, such studies have allowed an estimate to be made that 'one child in six or seven is being bullied in Australian schools with quite unacceptable frequency, that is, on a weekly basis or more often'.[5]

If one were to estimate (perhaps on an extrapolation of such figures) the number of people who have been affected by bullying behaviour in schools over the years, the result would, in all probability, be quite astonishing.

Is bullying behaviour in schools becoming more or less common? Certainly, our awareness of the issue is increasing, and this can only be a good thing. The only accurate way of testing whether school bullying is becoming more or less frequent is through repeated broad-scale surveys. Nationwide surveys are, however, expensive and time-consuming to conduct; frequently, resources have been (and some would argue, better) placed into the development of anti-bullying programmes for use in schools and school communities. Thankfully, a body of literature concerning this subject matter has been expanding over the last two decades. Some methods and techniques have been found to be helpful and effective in preventing and countering bullying behaviour in schools. Others – after they have been subjected to empirical testing by researchers, but far more often to the rigours of practical application in the schools and community situations – have been found wanting. And, of course, thinking around the subject area of anti-bullying has developed and changed over time. We both feel and hope that it is the better of the various anti-bullying methods and techniques that have been developed over the last two to three decades that have informed the practical content of this book.

Should anybody remain unconvinced about the serious nature of school bullying, let them consider the fact that in the year 2001, Neil Marr and Tim Field estimated that 16 children a year in the United Kingdom take their own lives, as a result of literally having been 'bullied to death'.[6] Hence, our ultimate challenge, as members of school communities, must be to work together in constructive ways in order that such heart-rending tragedies might be avoided. This book is an attempt to pinpoint what these constructive ways might be, and to support people in their endeavours to undertake effective anti-bullying work in school communities.

HOW TO USE THIS BOOK

The overall aim of this book is to provide school communities with the practical support and key to resources that they need in preventing and countering bullying and aggressive behaviour in schools. As the subtitle suggests, this book has been written primarily for practitioners as a training text. However, it is intended that every part of the school community – be these members of school management staff, members of classroom staff, parents of students, or students themselves – should potentially gain a great deal, in terms of practical understanding and advice, by reading at least certain sections of this book.

Accordingly, the main body of this book has been divided into four main sections (Chapters 2, 3, 4 and 5). Each of these chapters has as its target audience a different section of people within the school community. Each of these chapters begins with an overview of what is discussed in that chapter, and ends with a summary of the chapter, followed by a short list of further resources constructed with that section of people in mind. In Chapters 2, 3 and 4, a variety of suggestions for practical work have been included as 'Action suggestions', and appear as box diagrams within the text.

- *Chapter 2*: in this chapter, means by which anti-bullying work can be undertaken at the organizational/management level are outlined. This hinges largely upon anti-bullying policy within the school; hence, a step-by-step guide to formulating effective anti-bullying policy is included. Such a policy provides for the implementation of anti-bullying strategies, of which two main types are discussed: countering strategies (dealing with existing incidents of bullying and aggressive behaviour) and preventative strategies (reducing the likelihood of further incidences occurring). Countering strategies rest on means of effectively detecting, recording and intervening against bullying/aggressive behaviour (such as the 'no blame' approach), as well as the provision of resources and services for those who are affected (either as perpetrator, victim or bystander) by incidents of bullying/aggressive behaviour. Preventative strategies are concerned with the promotion of awareness of bullying, the promotion of pro-social behaviour, and the reduction of anti-social behaviour. Most of these strategies are practically realized through classroom work (hence, the bulk of the resources for these appear in Chapter 3), but must be underpinned through anti-bullying policy and school planning. Hence, these strategies are introduced in this chapter, and extensively cross-referenced throughout the rest of the book.

- *Chapter 3*: members of classroom staff are very much in the 'front line' concerning the practical aspects of dealing with and preventing bullying behaviour in schools. Unfortunately, members of classroom staff sometimes feel that their training has not always prepared them adequately for this role, and yet concerned parents will often require that teachers 'do something' about problems of bullying and aggressive behaviour. Hence, the bulk of this chapter is devoted to an attempt to supply teachers with the information and resources they need for effective anti-bullying classroom work. The strategies introduced in Chapter 2 (see above) – both countering and preventative strategies – are further elucidated, with an emphasis on classroom methods for promoting awareness and pro-social behaviour. This includes practical notes on implementing anti-bullying work through creative and discursive media. A critical focus, for reasons that are made apparent in this chapter, is self-esteem enhancement, and practical ideas for this type of work (and teaching practise) are outlined. The issue of workplace bullying and teachers is introduced and, whilst not covered in this book, the reader is referred to other helpful sources at this point.

- *Chapter 4*: parents are a critical group, in terms of anti-bullying efforts, because they often become aware of bullying problems before schools do (essentially, because bullied students are more likely to tell their parents than to report what they have suffered to teachers/principals). Parents also have a less formal role in schools than do other members of the school community. This chapter begins with a section entitled 'What parents need to know', and later focuses, for the most part, around practical advice for parents on what to do if their child is being bullied or is involved in bullying others. However, it is also necessary to focus on how parents and teachers can work together in terms of combating and preventing bullying behaviour – a collaborative approach (rather than the rather tragic scenario that sometimes evolves when teachers and parents end up blaming one another for the other's alleged 'inaction') is advanced as the key to doing this effectively.

- *Chapter 5*: this chapter is intended as a self-help guide for young people. It begins with a section entitled, 'What every young person needs to know about bullying'. Other sections, 'What to do if you are being bullied' and 'How to help prevent bullying in your school' are concerned with practical information for those involved in bullying behaviour – whether this is as a victim, bystander or perpetrator – and non-involved students. The chapter has been written with an older child or teenaged reader in mind; hence, the under-10s may need help from an adult in reading and understanding this chapter for themselves.

- The final part of this book, the 'Photocopiable Resources for Training', comprise resources for the practical training work of practitioners, in the form of sample Microsoft PowerPoint presentations that may be used in work with school management staff (Appendix A), in-service classroom staff training (Appendix B), and giving general talks to parents (Appendix

C) and students (Appendix D). Appendices A, B, C and D are based on, back up and are to be used in conjunction with the material of Chapters 2, 3, 4 and 5 respectively, and serve as means by which the key points of those chapters can be delivered to the specified target audience in the form of oral presentations.

Naturally, any given set of people within the school community will want to have a broader picture of bullying behaviour and anti-bullying work than is provided in 'their' chapter, and there are certain sets of core information that every group should know about. Hence, and also for the reason of avoiding repetition, notes on the appropriate use of cross-referencing to 'other' chapters have been included in the text.

As authors, we hope that we have succeeded in producing a readable and, above all, a usable book. We realize that no single book on the subject can ever be perfect, and that the increasing body of knowledge that exists concerning the issue of bullying and aggressive behaviour in schools means that (thankfully) new ideas and new approaches are being consistently generated. Additionally, our changing society means that our needs as people develop with the times – we are now at a point when we can and must universally condemn bullying, and not (as was the case in less enlightened years) merely accept it as being 'part of life', blinding ourselves to the often devastating consequences. So if we have missed out anything that should have been within our remit – if we, as the authors of this text, have not succeeded in picking up exactly what it was you, as a reader, hoped that you would gain from a so-titled text – then please let us know.

Chapter 2

Formulating an effective anti-bullying policy in schools

```
                 WHAT'S IN THIS CHAPTER
```

This chapter has been written primarily for those involved in school management – that is to say, policy-makers or reviewers or, regardless of his or her post, anyone involved in the day-to-day aspects of school management or school planning. With such personnel in mind, the following items have been included in this chapter:

- What school management staff need to know

- Formulating effective anti-bullying policy in schools

- Formulating effective anti-bullying strategies in schools.

Note for trainers and school management staff

In Appendices A–D, there are copies of sets of model slides (in Microsoft PowerPoint format) that might be used in:

1   discussion/planning and training work with school management personnel (Appendix A)

2   in-service training for teaching/non-teaching staff training (Appendix B)

3   talks with parents/members of the general public in the school community (Appendix C)

4   general talks with school students (Appendix D).

The information on these sets of slides is based on a condensation of the key points of Chapters 2 to 5 respectively.

WHAT SCHOOL MANAGEMENT STAFF NEED TO KNOW

How bullying is defined, and the forms it takes

Bullying has been defined in a number of ways over the years. Dan Olweus, the outstanding and original pioneer in the field of bullying research, defines it thus:

A person is being bullied when he or she is exposed, repeatedly and over time, to negative actions on the part of one or more other persons.[1]

In England, Peter Smith and Sonia Sharp have defined bullying simply, and very broadly, as:

the systematic abuse of power.[2]

In Scotland, the following definition has been used:

Bullying is long-standing violence, mental or physical, conducted by an individual or a group against an individual who is not able to defend himself or herself in that actual situation.[3]

And, finally, in the Republic of Ireland, the following definition is most often used:

Bullying is repeated aggression, verbal, psychological or physical, conducted by an individual or group against others.[4]

In bullying, as with other forms of aggressive behaviour, Peter Smith and David Thompson[5] note that the hurt that is done to the recipient is both intentional and unprovoked. However, it is important to distinguish between bullying and other forms of aggressive behaviour. This is usually done on the basis of the existence of an imbalance of power (be that power personal, social, or physical) – for whatever reason, the victim is relatively unable to defend herself or himself in the actual bullying situation – and repetition (one-off instances of aggression, whilst needing to be challenged, tend not to be categorized as bullying). However, it is the view of the authors that an isolated incident, such as a threat that is unjustified and serves to intimidate on an ongoing basis, can be described as bullying.

Bullying behaviour may take a variety of forms. What has been termed 'direct' bullying – where the victim is more or less openly attacked by the perpetrator – includes the categories of verbal bullying, physical bullying, gesture bullying, extortion and e-bullying (the sending of threatening or abusive material via electronic mail or text messages). 'Indirect' bullying is, to an extent, more covert, usually involving the deliberate manipulation of social relationships in order to socially isolate someone, or to make others dislike someone. This may include ignoring someone, and/or inducing others to do so; the spreading of malicious rumours, falsehoods or gossip; and the circulation of nasty notes, or the writing of insulting graffiti (on blackboards, or in public places). Bullying is a process, thus all aggressive acts must be challenged in order to interrupt the process.

Researchers have uncovered fairly consistent gender differences in the way in which males and females perpetrate bullying behaviour.[6] Whilst verbal bullying is generally the most commonly experienced form of bullying for male and female victims alike, male perpetrators are more likely than females to use physical means, whereas female perpetrators are more likely than males to use 'indirect' methods. As 'direct' bullying, or the results thereof, is often more evident than 'indirect' bullying, the latter may go undetected for relatively longer periods of time. Personnel at all-female or mixed gender schools may, of course, wish to take note of this point.

Throughout this book, we have endeavoured to use the term 'bully' as a verb, rather than as a noun. As labelling people 'bullies' is generally unhelpful, we instead refer to children/teenagers/young people who bully others/are engaged in bullying behaviour. This is not merely changing a grammatical convention: it reflects a change from the traditional (and ineffective) 'blame/punishment approach' (the seeking out and punishment of 'troublemakers') to the 'no blame approach' (which is discussed in some detail, below). The latter acknowledges that people who are involved in bullying, aggressive behaviour and harassment – whether as victims or perpetrators (or indeed, both) – need the support and intervention of the school community. Hence, those involved in bullying behaviour learn to take responsibility for their actions through the naming and challenging of inappropriate behaviour, the teaching of new skills, the promotion of insight and understanding, and the resolution of conflict.

The 'no blame' philosophy and approach[7]

The overcrowded prisons of many countries are testament to the fact that in the absence of rehabilitation, punishing wrongdoers does not reduce the incidence of the negative behaviour which they have perpetrated, nor reduce their likelihood of reoffending. Likewise, the school principal who earnestly believes that the student who has been suspended for bullying other students at school will spend the time for which he or she has been excluded first recognizing, then repenting, and finally making restitution for the error of his or her ways, is likely to be viewed at best as overly optimistic. It is perhaps more likely that such a student will view the suspension period as either a free holiday or an unfair sanction taken against him or her by someone who is, for now, in a more powerful position and has used that power unfairly. The student now feels abused, and thus vengeful – and is only too aware that what made his or her predicament, if it is viewed as such, was the report of someone who was after all less powerful than him or her. In short, any 'blame-punishment' system is inherently flawed, as its focus is on attributing blame, and the labelling of individuals as deviant. It also exercises power perceived as legitimate against power perceived as illegitimate (by the 'authority', but not by the blamed individual, whose perceptions are likely to be precisely the reverse), and stands in ignorance of our essential human capacities for insight, accepting responsibility for one's own behaviour, learning and change.

'No blame' does not mean 'no responsibility'; rather, the opposite. In addressing the process – in separating, at the initial point of intervention, actions from actors – we look for constructive and rehabilitative solutions. If I aggress against you, and someone punishes me, I first deny my anti-social behaviour, and then feel justified in it, and in myself. As we've seen above, if I get at you, and then I perceive you getting someone to get at me, then rest assured, I'll get you back – along with, perhaps in an indirect way, whoever you got to get at me. But what if you could put your need for vengeance aside, and whoever was in authority could put aside their need to (be seen to?) do something to maintain order, and I was, instead of being castigated, encouraged to look at how my behaviour affected you? After all, I might not know, or I might know but not have cared – but I could be given the chance to learn something valuable. I might, for example, be able to think through what I've done, and look at possible consequences. Is what I'm doing likely to lead to something favourable for me and you? Or is it hurting you and yours and, ultimately, likely to end up causing hurt for me and mine? Given the same situation occurring again, could I do something different? If I can't see other options now, could I learn some? How would this work out instead?

The 'no blame' philosophy, then, is really one of common sense, but offers us a way to escape from the 'violence begets violence' cycle. Practically implementing this philosophy is not always immediately apparent, so considerable attention is given to this in the 'Formulating effective anti-bullying policy in schools' and 'Formulating effective anti-bullying strategies in schools' sections below.

Bullying behaviour as a school community issue

If research from the 1970s and 1980s onwards is generally reckoned to have promoted an awareness amongst educators of the scale and seriousness of bullying behaviour amongst school students, then similar work from the 1990s and 2000s has made an inroad into promoting such an awareness amongst the general public of the scale and seriousness of bullying behaviour in the workplace. If we are to conceptualize the word 'bully' as a verb, not a noun, we must see bullying as an activity, rather than a stereotypical role; and if we are to follow the implications of the 'no blame' approach (see above), as well as the evidence of our eyes and ears, we must conclude that anyone within the school community may become involved in bullying and aggressive behaviour, either as a perpetrator or as a victim.

Thus, as the traditional conception of bullying as being manifested in physical violence is only part of the whole story, so too is focusing exclusively on the student–student dyadic relationship. Student-on-student bullying is, indeed, unfortunately quite commonplace, and gradually becoming more effectively researched; however, the 'whole story' also depends on our recognizing staff-on-student bullying, student-on-staff bullying, staff-on-staff bullying, parent-on-staff bullying, and so on. When one considers that the most developmentally immature people within the school community – the students – are, during the school years, in a critical period of the formation of social attitudes, and are likely to learn their attitudes towards violence and persecution from their teachers and their parents, as well as from their peers, the importance of addressing bullying and aggressive behaviour at a school community level is readily apparent. It would be unrealistic for a teacher to expect the students under his or her care to take an anti-bullying message he or she delivers seriously, when his or her conduct towards either students or staff colleagues is characterized by abuse, aggression or harassment.

First and foremost, we see bullying as an unacceptable form of interpersonal behaviour. Unfortunately, in years gone by, adults have shirked their responsibility of intervening against bullying, and perpetrators of this behaviour have seen their actions ignored or, worse still, legitimized instead of being condemned. Such a pattern is also evident when we look at other examples of abusive behaviour: racism, child labour, colonial aggression and slavery were all once seen as part of the natural order of things. As these latter have become universally condemned, so too should any form of bullying, aggressive behaviour and harassment in the school (and, indeed, wider community).

FORMULATING EFFECTIVE ANTI-BULLYING POLICY IN SCHOOLS

Issues to be aware of

If we view bullying behaviour as a school community issue (see above), we are compelled to ask ourselves a number of questions:

- *Who will take the responsibility* for drafting, reviewing and finalizing the anti-bullying policy statement? And who will take responsibility for implementing the various aspects of strategy and so on, specified in the anti-bullying policy statement?

- *What are our overall goals* for the anti-bullying policy? Do we wish to find ways to deal with the bullying behaviour we have, or to prevent future incidents occurring – or both?

- *Are we specifically interested in bullying behaviour*, or should the policy seek to address related issues such as aggressive behaviour, and harassment? Or even a wider issue such as indiscipline?

- *Who should anti-bullying policy and strategies within a school serve?* Should this be the students only? Or both students and staff? Or even students, staff and parents? If one casts one's net wider, who should, or has the authority and responsibility to, implement it?

- How can we find practical ways of involving the teaching and non-teaching staff, students and parents in the policy formation process? To what extent do they take the issue of school bullying seriously? Can I assume that everyone conceptualizes bullying in the same way, and is convinced of the necessity to address it in school? (The answer to this is 'no'.) Can I expect them to be sufficiently motivated to contribute towards anti-bullying work? If so, how may they be so motivated? Can I at least assume that all the members of the teaching staff are 'singing from the same hymn sheet'? (Again, the answer to this – in the absence of a well worked through anti-bullying policy and attendant set strategies – is likely to be 'no').

- What are the key legal, curricular and policy issues that I should be aware of before publishing an anti-bullying policy statement? How will this policy tie in with other policies already in existence within the school?

Essentially, the greater the extent to which one can satisfy oneself regarding these questions before work on an anti-bullying policy begins in earnest, the smoother the policy formation process is likely to be. As consultation and collaboration with the school community is absolutely key to the eventual success of anti-bullying policy and strategy within the school, a separate section on this now follows.

Consultation and collaboration with the school community

In order for people to feel ownership over a policy directive, they need to have been consulted. Too often, the responsibility for directing school policy lies with the school management authorities, and the realization of such policy with the school principal. Thus, students, teachers and parents end up feeling that this policy (which usually 'binds' them in some way, usually in the form of a school rule that the students must follow) 'comes down from above', and they have little or nothing to do with it. We have set out our view that bullying behaviour can involve and affect anyone within a school community; therefore, everyone should be part of the 'solution'. Hence, we prefer a model of the school management facilitating/driving the policy formation process, into which all interest groups have (at least the chance to provide) input.

In our work with schools on anti-bullying policy formation, the authors have found some types of working formats to be successful (see sections immediately below). As noted at the beginning of the chapter, Appendices A–D consist of copies of sets of model slides (based on the key points of Chapters 2 to 5 respectively) that might be used in discussions/training with (1) school management personnel (Appendix A); (2) staff in-service development (Appendix B); (3) parents/community members (Appendix C); and, (4) students (Appendix D).

All these groups will require input as to what bullying behaviour is (that is, how it may be defined), the forms that bullying behaviour can take, the 'no blame' philosophy, the fact that bullying behaviour is best conceptualized as a community issue, and the various ideas that exist around investigating, recording, countering and preventing bullying behaviour in schools and the necessity of doing so. Above all, it is important to recognize – as the authors have attempted to reflect in the course of this book – that these groups of people will have different levels of knowledge, beliefs, feelings and concerns about bullying behaviour. Some people will refuse to recognize bullying behaviour as an issue. Some people will refuse to accept that time and resources should be given over to such a matter. Some people believe in the 'old myths' around bullying behaviour – that it is part of life, unavoidable, that 'boys will be boys', that it somehow builds character – 'I was boxed over the ears by the senior boys every day, and devil the bit of harm it ever did me'. Some people are unaware that their own behaviour is aggressive, or is bullying in nature – and some people are well aware of this, and would like free rein to continue.

Equally, there are some people who are so concerned about the slightest possibility of inequity and injustice in the school community that they unfortunately conceptualize incidents that cannot legitimately be classified as acts of bullying as being so. For example, it is not bullying when a teacher makes fair and just criticism of a student's work or, after investigating a student's alleged wrongdoing to the satisfaction of all concerns, finds it necessary to discipline a child in accordance with the discipline policy of the school – no matter how bitter and vocal the student's complaints are. Yet, if efforts around anti-bullying policy and strategies are to be effective, each individual member of the school community must be at least invited 'to the table', and her or his voice must be heard.

Naturally, the precise nature of work to be undertaken will depend on how far the school has already progressed in its anti-bullying work. Where no anti-bullying work has been undertaken, the critical thing is immediately to start awareness-raising work throughout the school community, with the goal of forming and disseminating an anti-bullying policy statement and an attendant set of strategies. Some schools may be relatively advanced in their anti-bullying work, in which case, review and evaluation of the effectiveness of an already operational policy and strategies may be warranted (with, perhaps, extra attention being given to creative preventative work, if countering strategies are found to be effective). But however expert a school feels itself to be, there is – and must always be – scope for evaluation and revision (see section below – 'Building-in and implementing evaluation and review measures').

Action suggestion 2.1: working with school management staff

People   Trainer, school management staff (colleagues)

Materials   This entire chapter, along with the complementary Appendix A; overhead/data projector; flip chart

Methods   Trainers and planners need to acknowledge that individual members of school management staff may differ as to their expertise and perspectives on, and motivation towards, undertaking anti-bullying work. Thus, whilst round-table planning sessions may be a typical way in which work with generally expert individuals such as management staff is undertaken, more general awareness work (implemented, say, by an individual with particular expertise in the area of anti-bullying work) may be a helpful precursor.

Action suggestion 2.2: working with classroom staff

People   Trainer, school classroom staff

Materials   Selected (see notes below) material from this chapter and Chapter 3; Appendix B; overhead/data projector; flip chart

Methods   Teaching staff are, in our experience, less concerned (although not necessarily less interested) with the theoretical side of students' involvement in bullying behaviour than with learning practical ways by which such behaviour can be dealt with in the school in general, and in the classroom in the 'here and now' in particular. Teachers are very much in the 'front line' concerning the practical aspects of dealing with bullying behaviour in schools but, unfortunately, teachers have sometimes (rather courageously) informed us that whilst their training has not always adequately prepared them for this role, concerned parents will often require that teachers 'do something' about problems of bullying and aggressive behaviour.

A typical in-service training session might last for half a school day (say, up to two-and-a-half hours of input/training exercises/discussion, plus breaks as necessary). As well as the material that every school community group needs to know (see above), input concerning the following issues should be given:

1 *The 'no blame' philosophy* and its practical application (see above, section 'The "no blame" philosophy and approach', and below, section 'Formulating effective anti-bullying strategies in schools').

2 *Countering strategies* (to include how these are underpinned by the anti-bullying policy statement) (see below, section 'Countering strategies', and Chapter 3, section 'Dealing with incidents of bullying behaviour').

3 *Preventative strategies* (see below, section 'Preventative strategies', and Chapter 3, section 'Preventative strategies: ideas for classroom activities').

4 *Achieving consensus*. For any school rule, policy or programme to 'work', that is to say, for it to be effectively implemented by the staff, the majority of the staff must 'buy into' it. In terms of harassment, bullying and aggressive behaviour, it is absolutely essential that all the teaching and non-teaching staff are 'singing from the same hymn sheet'. Thus, if no anti-bullying policy statement exists at the time of working with the teaching staff, a good way to start work is to try to generate a definition of bullying upon which all staff members are agreed (and if an anti-bullying policy statement does exist, a good way to start work is by reviewing the existing definition's strengths and weaknesses). The definitions mentioned at the beginning of this chapter can serve as models.

As 'bullying' has now become a bit of a 'buzzword' – it seems like ten years ago, the popular psychological buzzword was 'stress' – it may be indiscriminately used, or even deliberately misused. For this reason, some schools have found it necessary to be very clear not only about what bullying is, but also about what bullying is not (this point underlines again the importance of definitional issues). For example, young children may feel (and say) that they have been bullied when something they do not like happens to them (regardless of power imbalance, repetition, whether the hurt was intentional, and so on). Thus, the child might accuse a teacher who has, say, fairly disciplined the child, of bullying him or her! So some schools have added statements such as, 'it is not bullying when a teacher offers fair and just criticism of a students' work' to the definition of bullying outlined in the anti-bullying policy statement.

Naturally, consensus should also be aimed at *vis-à-vis* all aspects of the countering and preventative strategies specified in the anti-bullying policy statement. This, of course, can be time-consuming, but bringing out the attitudes towards and beliefs about bullying behaviour held by school management and classroom staff can, if properly and sensitively facilitated, be a very fruitful exercise in itself. In the authors' experience, conducting small-group structured exercises around fictional

CONTINUED

scenarios of bullying behaviour has been an effective way of elucidating such opinions in a constructive way.

5 *Who should the policy serve?* It should, of course, be remembered that as bullying behaviour is a community issue, the rather delicate issue of workplace bullying and teachers should be broached (staff on staff bullying), as well as the issues of staff-on-student, and student-on-staff harassment, bullying and aggressive behaviour. If it is decided that anti-bullying policy and strategy in the school should serve adults as well as students, the input of teachers will, of course, be invaluable (see Chapter 3, section 'A brief note on classroom staff and bullying behaviour in the workplace').

Action suggestion 2.3: working with parents

People   Trainer, parents of the school's students, members of the wider local school community

Materials   Material from Chapter 4, and Appendix C; overhead/data projector; flip chart

Methods   Parents are a critical group, in terms of anti-bullying efforts, because they often become aware of bullying problems before schools do (essentially, because bullied students are more likely to tell their parents what they have suffered than to report this to teachers/principals). Parents also have a less formal role in schools than do other members of the school community. In our experience, parents often are in need of, or are most interested in, sound practical advice on what to do if their child is being bullied or is involved in bullying others. However, it is also necessary to focus on how parents and teachers can work together in terms of combating and preventing bullying behaviour. A collaborative approach (rather than the rather tragic scenario that sometimes evolves when teachers and parents end up blaming one another for the other's alleged 'inaction') is key to doing this effectively.

Parents, either through a meeting of an existing parent-teacher association/Parents' Council or otherwise, are often quite amenable to attending evening talks presented by an internal or external speaker. Such a talk might typically be of approximately one-and-a-half hours' length (say, from 7.30 p.m. until 9.00 p.m.), and consist of up to one hour's input from the speaker, and half an hour's 'open floor' questions from the audience. The material of Chapter 4, and its complementary Appendix C, can provide trainers and school management staff with guidelines as to the material that such a presentation should include. There are certain issues that one should hold in mind:

1 *Scheduling*. Very few people will attend anything scheduled for a Friday evening, whether they 'have plans' or not. Also, and at the risk of indulging in gender stereotypes, we have found that televised sporting events can hinder fathers' attendance.

2 *Location*. In schools where there is a weak or negative relationship between the staff and the students' parents, remember that parental non-involvement in after-school activities may be due to the parents' own negative experiences of schooling in childhood. Consequently, the last place such a parent is likely to want to spend his or her spare time is in a school, no matter how worthy the cause. If such a pattern is in evidence, consider hosting the meeting outside school (say, in a church hall or a community centre).

3 *Ongoing issues of bullying behaviour*, that a presenter may not be aware of, may cloud the interactive aspects of an evening talk. For instance, it may be that a parent in the audience has a child who has been bullied, and feels that the school has not dealt with this effectively: what may result is the parent's anger and disappointment leading him or her to try to make a point, or score points off, the school in the form of the presenter or any attendant school staff members. A presenter can do one of two things: first, ensure that he or she is kept fully informed of any recent/current cases in the school; or secondly, and we think per-haps more realistically and importantly, set a 'boundary' about what the evening talk can reasonably encompass. For example: 'I'd like to discuss a few points about harassment, bullying and aggressive behav-iour with you this evening. I do realize that these are sometimes sensitive issues, so what I'd ask is that we keep the talk and any ques-tions you might have as general as possible, and leave aside for this evening anything specific that's affecting you or your children/teenagers at the moment. If you do need any specific help, I think it might be more effective to discuss this in a one-to-one context, rather than in a meeting like this. So if this is the case, please contact me personally – I'll give you my contact details at the end of the talk.'

4 *Harassment, bullying and aggressive behaviour are sensitive issues*, and a parent may have questions that he or she wants to be answered, but is unwilling to ask these questions in a public forum. Thus, an 'open door' should always be provided – perhaps in the form of the presenter giving out his or her contact details at the end of the presentation (a small flyer prevents the problem of 'writing down').

Action suggestion 2.4: awareness work with students

People   Trainer, the school's students, members of wider local school community

Materials Material from Chapter 5, and Appendix D; overhead/data projector; flip chart; materials for art and creative work

Methods   In the context of making a short presentation to school students, a good deal can be achieved; but what the methods by which this work may be achieved will very much depend on the age of the school students involved. Nevertheless, it is possible to make some general recommendations. First and foremost, trainers are encouraged to use their own creativity in order to facilitate, in turn, the creativity of the students. In this way, creativity can serve as a tool by which the anti-bullying message can be 'brought home' as unambiguously as is possible.

1 *Set out practical parameters*. Working with one class at a time, for a class period or two's duration, is probably the most manageable set-up. It can be helpful, in terms of classroom management, to work with the class's teacher in a co-teaching set-up.

2 *Use of 'circle time', or similar teaching method*. Where this is in place in school, or the class are used to such a set-up, or can quickly adapt to it, a 'circle time' seating arrangement and method of working is extremely helpful in fostering a discursive atmosphere. In any event, it is important that as many students as possible contribute to the discussion; take questions and suggestions from as many different students as you can; as in any teaching situation, it is important to be gentle in encouraging quieter class members and limiting the more vocal ones! Due to the sensitivity of the issue of bullying – remember, in talking to any class group, it is a statistical probability that you will be addressing several people who have been victimized, and several who have been involved in the bullying of others – it is important that one sets boundaries. So a few ground rules like 'don't mention any names or specific incidents that have happened to people in this room', 'only say what you feel comfortable saying' and the like might be helpful.

3 *Use a combination of teaching strategies*. With very young children in mind, it should be recalled that the attention span of students can be quite limited (especially the more abstract the concept gets); hence, if one wants to focus on the issue of bullying for a prolonged period, one will have to include a variety of methods by which to do so, or the audience is likely to 'drift'. Some facilitators like to start with an 'ice-breaker', such as showing a film or film extract (a short list of such resources is available at the end of this book). Others like to mobilize the children physically, by playing

CONTINUED

some 'get to know you' games (ideas on this are included in Chapter 3, section 'Preventative strategies: ideas for classroom activities'). However, there must always be some input from the facilitator; this is best done by putting questions to the students, rather than lecturing to them. Naturally, the facilitator must manage the process, and to some extent steer the students towards a pro-social and anti-bullying standpoint. Some important questions to ask the students might be as follows (naturally, the wording of these questions and the number used will depend on the age and understanding level of the students involved):

(a) What is bullying? What forms does it take?

(b) How is bullying different to other forms of aggressive behaviour?

(c) Is calling names, or using nicknames bullying? What sort of names should never be used?

(d) What do you think is the worst sort of bullying? Why?

(e) How do people feel when they are bullied?

(f) Why do people bully others? Especially if they know that it's wrong to do so?

(g) What could you do if you/your friend/someone else was being bullied?

(h) What could you do if your friend(s) was (were) involved in bullying others?

(i) Why do you think people don't tell when they are being bullied? What could you/the school/parents do to help someone in this position to come forward?

(j) How can the members of this class look out for each other, to make sure this class is 'bully free'?

Some creative activity should then follow, followed by further discussion, in which the key points that emerged from the first discussion are reiterated, in a form that the students can understand. If one can get the anti-bullying message down to three or four points that the young people themselves have raised, then the material is likely to 'hit home'.

4 *Use of age-appropriate creative activities.* Here, the facilitator's imagination (and resources) are the only real limit – creative activities that have been successfully employed in this sort of work have included drawing, model-making, sculpture, posters, role-play (used by some, although the authors do not recommend this due to issues of sensitivity and possible 'fallout'), scripted original drama (find a task for everyone!), games and structured

exercises, the examination of text/poetry, and the development of charters. Details on how these may be realized (particularly the use of charters) are included in Chapter 3. The important thing is to match the activity to the age and ability level of the students − if the 'right' message is to be sent out consistently, even the intellectually weakest student should be able to participate fully in whatever is going on. For much the same reason, facilitators should always be prepared to 'join in', and not simply to set the tasks. Interestingly, one's own artistic ineptitude can be a great help to the facilitator − if you are not afraid to put your unrecognizable sculpture on display, neither will the students be − and what better demonstration of 'it's the taking part that counts' could be possible?

5 It is important to *put the creative work done by students in such sessions on public display*. Drawings and written material can be put into folders to create 'books' and 'magazines'; models, sculptures and posters can be put on display in classrooms and corridors; role-plays can be expanded into plays to be performed; charters can be put on display and into general use. Naturally, all such created material should be on display in an 'anti-bullying week' (see below, 'Action suggestion 2.5').

6 *The importance of this type of classroom anti-bullying work*. As well as fostering increased awareness, the first time that this sort of work is done with a class an invaluable opportunity is provided for the uptake of students' ideas with a view to anti-bullying policy and strategy formation (the construction of 'class charters' being an especially valuable tool). Subsequently, of course, work of this nature, and sessions of the type described above, can form part of ongoing preventative anti-bullying work done in a school.

7 *Peer mediation and peer mentorship*. Some schools have introduced 'peer mediation', in which (usually) more senior students are trained as mediators in disputes and problems between the younger students, or are assigned to younger (usually, incoming) students in a 'buddying' system (mentorship), helping them with their day-to-day adjustment in school. Peer mentors should not be expected or encouraged to 'deal with' incidents of bullying − this should always be the responsibility of classroom staff. In the event of their younger 'buddies' being bullied, peer mentors can best assist by helping the bullied student to find the confidence to report the bullying behaviour to the relevant school authorities.

General points concerning countering strategy work with students are included in this chapter, below (see section 'Countering strategies'). Further ideas for classroom work with students to be undertaken by classroom staff are included in Chapter 3, section 'Preventative strategies: ideas for classroom activities'.

Establishing measures for dissemination, promotion and evaluation

Disseminating and promoting the policy

A school should be proud of taking a proactive stance against bullying behaviour. To act publicly against bullying behaviour is not an admission of past problems; it is, rather, a statement that the school is finding practical ways to safeguard the people of the community of which it is a part. One way in which this message can be underlined is by displaying the finished product of the anti-bullying policy formation process – that is, the written policy statement – as publicly as is possible (rather in the manner of a charter). The written anti-bullying policy statement should be construed as a matter of public record, and available in a user-friendly form for consultation by anyone in the school community at their request. It should therefore be displayed on all school notice boards as a permanent poster, and available to all school students in a language that they can understand. The statement should also be given to all members of staff (especially new and non-permanent members) and all parents (especially parents who are 'new' to the school community, that is, whose children have just entered the school), perhaps at the beginning of each academic year. The statement could also usefully be distributed to all relevant groups in the wider local community (local police, youth groups, centres of religious worship, child, family and health centres, sports clubs and so on).

Building-in and implementing evaluation and review measures

Remember that a written anti-bullying policy statement is not an end in itself, but a working document that should be regularly reviewed, and updated as necessary. It is useful to acknowledge this latter fact within the written anti-bullying policy statement. Evaluation measures can take the form of formalised research projects, involving pre- and post-measure questionnaire comparisons. However, given the resources (including time resources) that most schools have at their disposal, the integration of less formalized feedback from the various groups within the school community is a more realistic methodology.

It makes sense to set aside time to review anti-bullying policy and strategy within the school – say, on an annual basis, at general staff meetings. Parents councils may also wish to set aside time to review the policy, and provide input into the policy; additionally, the preventative work done by students in school also provides a formalized way for them to make an input or express their opinions. Patterns of bullying are to some extent 'fluid' within a school community – it is quite possible that in one month, discipline issues might be non-existent, and yet this may be followed the next month by (say) a spate of text-message bullying. Additionally, individuals' different psychosocial positions within the school community – management staff, classroom staff, parents and students – give members of these groups different contact with, concerns about and perspectives on bullying behaviour and its countering and prevention. In terms of integrating ideas for the review of anti-bullying policy and strategy, an 'open door' practise should, as far as is practicable, be maintained – essentially, each point, raised by whomsoever within the school community, should be given due consideration.

FORMULATING EFFECTIVE ANTI-BULLYING STRATEGIES IN SCHOOLS

Countering strategies

A complete anti-bullying policy should include directives for both countering strategies – dealing with any current incidents of bullying behaviour in the school – and preventative strategies (see below). As stated above (see above, 'Action suggestion 2.2'), it is important that a consensus is achieved amongst the classroom and management staff (that is to say, those involved in the practical and day-to-day implementation) as to all details of these strategies during the anti-bullying policy formation process and in subsequent anti-bullying work in school. Countering strategies should include means by which incidents of bullying behaviour may be reported, investigated and recorded, and sanctions and supports for those involved in incidents of bullying behaviour.

Specifying how incidents of alleged bullying behaviour are to be reported, investigated and recorded

The key to effective anti-bullying work in school is to encourage those who are victims of and, perhaps even more importantly, witnesses to incidents of bullying behaviour to come forward and report the victimization that they have either suffered or witnessed. However, there is often quite an enormous social and peer group pressure against coming forward. A complainant, no matter how legitimate his or her grievance, may be castigated by his or her peers for 'grassing', 'clyping', 'ratting' or 'snitching' – all regional variants of a quite dreadful label: a label that immediately pathologizes the pro-social behaviour of the complainant, and may be sufficient to outgroup him or her from his or her peers permanently. A profound reluctance on the part of bullied students to report the bullying they have suffered has been evident in all of the large-scale surveys of bullying behaviour in schools conducted to date (for examples, see those cited in note 6). The reasons for this have not been fully elucidated to date; it may be reasonably assumed that a child will want to avoid the damning label of 'grass', 'clype', 'rat' or 'snitch'.

It may also be the case, as a qualitative study of primary school children's attitudes towards and feelings about bullying behaviour has to an extent demonstrated,[8] that bullied children fear retribution from their aggressors should they break the 'playground code of silence', or are unaware or somehow doubtful of their school's ability to address the issue in a way that protects their safety. In any event, encouraging school students to report bullying is an uphill struggle. The first stage in that struggle, it is suggested, is to facilitate the process of reporting as much as is possible. By and large, school students know that they should report bullying; they need to feel that it is safe for them to do so. If an effective and transparent set of means by which incidents of bullying behaviour may be dealt with is evident to all members of the school community, then the students' confidence in the fact that the reporting of bullying is both safe and desirable can be promoted.

Steps towards means by which incidents may be investigated and recorded are as follows:

1   *Co-ordination of anti-bullying countering strategies.* Some schools have found it helpful to nominate an individual staff member, or small group of members, who are responsible for the co-ordination of anti-bullying strategies within the school. Here, voluntarism is probably the best means of selection; having stated this, it is of course advisable that the co-ordinator should be a permanent and senior member of staff. The responsibilities of the co-ordinator will be to implement the points outlined immediately below; hence, the staff body (who should all be involved in the selection of the co-ordinator) should choose an individual who has the abilities to meet these. Other schools have preferred to share the responsibilities amongst all staff. This being said, all members of classroom and management staff should be sufficiently prepared and resourced to permit that any student may report an incident of bullying behaviour to any member of staff.

2   *Talks to the whole student body.* Periodically, and when the opportunity presents itself to address the entire school body – and preferably at least once a term – students should be reminded that the school has an active anti-bullying policy, and that bullying behaviour is not accepted in this school. Some headteachers have also used such talks to 'depathologize' reporting – saying something along the lines of, 'This is a telling school. At some schools, students don't always tell their teachers when something is going on that they're not happy about. But in this school, we do tell – and we look out for each other by telling a teacher when we know about some-one else being bullied, or we are being bullied ourselves'.

3   *The essentials of reporting.* When someone makes an allegation of having been bullied, or reports that someone else has been bullied, the most impor-tant thing (in the initial phases) is to attend to that person's safety needs. Communicating that we 'believe' the complainant is perhaps too strong – after all, individuals' perceptions will differ, and not every incident is unam-biguous – but we should communicate that we accept what the complainant has to say. The complainant's statements should be listened to actively; and with no interpretation, the complainant's specific grievances – particularly those concerning concrete events – should be recorded in writing, and kept on record. Some schools have found it helpful to introduce the use of stan-dardized reporting forms for these purposes.

4   *Talks/interviews with those involved in bullying behaviour*. Alleged perpetrators and victims should be interviewed separately; where a gang has been involved in bullying, the members should be interviewed separately before they are interviewed together. It is advisable to investigate the matter as soon as is possible, in order to prevent further instances occurring, and to prevent the opportunity for alleged perpetrators to arrange the 'reconstruction' of their own (and others') versions of events. Remember, it is extremely helpful to talk to any potential witnesses of the alleged incident, as well as to those who are alleged to be the perpetrators of the incident: people's perspectives will vary. When talking to alleged perpetrators, remember that an accusatory tone is not helpful, and that the alleged perpetrator should be assured that you will listen to his or her side of things before any decision is made. Note that it is not necessary to tell the alleged perpetrator who has reported the incident – after all, it could be the victim, a bystander, a parent, or indeed anyone within the school community who has merely heard about the incident. It is only necessary to convey that an alleged incident has come to the attention of the school authorities, and that bullying behaviour is not tolerated within the school.

It is advocated that serious talks are held with those who, on investigation of the matter, have been found to be responsible for perpetrating incidents of bullying behaviour. The essential things are to (a) safeguard the victim of the bullying behaviour; and, (b) prevent future recurrences of the bullying behaviour; these should be kept in mind, rather than the simple application of sanctions. Where the relative severity of the act and school discipline policy deems this possible, it is desirable that the perpetrator is given one (and only one) chance to take responsibility for, and adapt, his or her behaviour (after all, in some cases, it is a genuine possibility that the perpetrator literally did not know that his or her behaviour could be construed or was experienced by the victim as bullying).

Essentially, the perpetrator needs to be informed – in good faith – of three things: (a) that his or her behaviour constituted an unambiguous incident of bullying behaviour, and that this is in breach of the school's anti-bullying policy; (b) that he or she must refrain from bullying, and the specific forms of bullying behaviour experienced by the victim, in future; and, (c) that sanctions (as specified in the anti-bullying policy statement, in line with the school's overall discipline code) will be implemented should he or she further transgress any aspects of the school's anti-bullying policy, and that any acts of retribution against the victim will be dealt with by the severest possible application of these sanctions.

5   *The role of parents*. Pikas, the originator of the 'Farsta' method,[9] upon which the 'no blame approach' is largely based, discourages the involvement of parents in the schools' dealing with incidents of bullying behaviour. The message that students are able to take responsibility for, and where necessary modify, their own behaviour is consistently emphasized. Elsewhere, Olweus

informs us that in his lengthy experience (which is second to none), parents can be a valuable resource. It is possible that this contradiction does not need to pose an impasse. After all, this lack of consensus amongst the experts opens the way for the school management staff to consider for themselves whether in their specific situation the school's students' parents will indeed be a valuable resource or not. Is the school's relationship with the parent body healthy enough to make use of parents as a resource in this way? Alternatively, if the relationship has not been positive to date, would this type of an involvement prove to be a 'Trojan horse' by which the parents' involvement in other school matters could be encouraged? Do we find Pikas's approach here to be absolutely convincing? Or, noting the interchange between acts of bullying behaviour in the local community (that is, outside the school gates/school hours) and in the school, is it more helpful to have the parents 'on board' during this process? The school management staff, in consultation with members of the other groups within the school community, must decide. It should also be noted that informing parents of incidents of bullying behaviour allows parents to open up a dialogue with the child on the subject and, with help from the school's awareness programme, identify factors that may be causative of bullying. This will give parents an opportunity to examine the stress factors that may be triggering the aggressive behaviours. Naturally, where the law and policy dictate that parents should be involved in the school's dealing with incidents of their child's/teenager's indiscipline, this must, of course, be followed.

Schools should, of course, be aware that when parents hear that their child/teenager has been bullied (more often than not, after the young person has kept his or her victimization a secret for months or even years) that they will want the school to take swift and summary action. Whereas dealing with an incident of bullying is time consuming, it is imperative to keep parents who bring a complaint as informed as is practically possible about the progress a school is making in dealing with the case.

Specifying sanctions and support systems for those involved in bullying behaviour

Some schools have found it helpful to introduce written behavioural contracts in dealing with incidents of bullying behaviour. Typically, the perpetrator is asked to sign to the fact that in future he or she will refrain from the incidents of bullying behaviour that have been alleged against him or her; that he or she understands the nature of the sanctions that will be applied should he transgress the school's anti-bullying policy in future; and that he or she agrees to be bound by this agreement. Finally, the date and time of a follow-up interview should be scheduled – be it in a week or a month's time, depending on the severity of the situation – which the perpetrator agrees to attend. This behavioural contract must be signed by the anti-bullying co-ordinator and/or relevant member of staff and the perpetrator, and can be so designed that it may be counter-signed by the student's class tutor, year head, parent(s) or guardian(s), and senior school management staff as necessary.

Anyone who has dealt with investigating a case of bullying behaviour will, of course, be very mindful of the incredible length of time that it can take to 'get to the bottom' of things – how one student's story will contradict another; how stories will change over time; how some perpetrators of bullying behaviour will refuse outright to accept that they said or did anything at all. In a way, the use of standardized behavioural contract forms is liberating here. For example, the perpetrator may stand accused of (say) calling his victim nasty names, spreading rumours about the victim's family and physically hurting the victim in some way. It may be that in fact the perpetrator was responsible for name-calling and physical bullying only, and that the rumours came from a different source. However, the perpetrator in this incidence is not signing an admission of his guilt to all of these events – he is simply signing to say that he will refrain from perpetrating such incidents in future; and, if one has not done something in the past, then logically it should pose no difficulties to keep on not doing it. There are, of course, a few problems with this, but some schools have found that the implementation of such a system frees the member of staff from the consistent round of accusation and counter-accusation and – here is the most important thing – the process of ensuring the future safety of the victimized student is significantly speeded up. The use of standardized behavioural forms, of course, ensures that every member of staff can deal with incidents of bullying behaviour in exactly the same concrete way, and that a record of this action is automatically recorded.

As indicated above, all aspects of dealing with incidents of bullying behaviour must be in keeping with all other aspects of the school's overall discipline policy. This will include the specification of sanctions to be taken in response to transgressions of the school's anti-bullying policy. It is essential that considerable care is given to this aspect of the anti-bullying policy formation, and that (once again) consensus amongst all school staff is achieved regarding this matter. The reader is reminded that the anti-bullying policy must conform to all legal, curricular and policy directives that are operational in the school community and wider environment.

In terms of support services, the school must summon up (and specify) whatever resources it may have, or can reasonably accrue. It is not as simple as pointing out that the school has a counselling service (or similar) and that victims of bullying should present themselves there. Counselling is, in some cases, useful, but is not a panacea in terms of dealing with those involved in bullying behaviour. There is much that can be done by classroom and school management staff (largely in terms of social skills training) where opportunities present themselves: a perpetrator may need to learn how to manage anger, and to develop empathy or interpersonal skills; the so-called 'provocative victim' may need to accrue appropriate social skills; and mediation can be extremely useful, as can (in a preventative sense) mentorship schemes. Again, it is a case of putting together a package of resources, and taking the opportunity to use such resources wisely and appropriately. Further details on these practical means of working with such resources are provided in Chapter 3, section 'Preventative strategies: ideas for classroom activities'.

Preventative strategies

Some ideas for the use of preventative strategies (for example, awareness work) have been suggested above (see section 'Action suggestion 2.4'. Further ideas are provided in Chapter 3, section 'Preventative strategies: ideas for classroom activities'. Space does not permit for these to be restated here; however, the reader is very much encouraged to refer to these sections.

Action suggestion 2.5: holding an 'anti-bullying week'

People   Trainer, all of the members of the school community (school management staff, teaching staff, parents of your school's students, your school's students), members of the wider local school community

Materials   All necessary materials for the creative work undertaken by pupils; all necessary training and information materials for work with classroom staff, parents and students; multiple copies of the school's anti-bullying policy statement

Methods   Some schools have found it helpful to launch their newly formed anti-bullying policy, or indeed start new terms or academic years, with an 'anti-bullying week'. Creative work done by students (see above, section 'Action suggestion 2.4') may be put on public display; dramatic and musical performances may be held; evening talks/open days/information evenings can be held for parents (see above, 'Action suggestion 2.3'), and in-service training (perhaps by an external consultant) can be held for classroom staff (see above, Action suggestion 2.2'). The imagination and organizational abilities of the school management staff and the designated anti-bullying co-ordinator are the only limits!

SUMMARY

- In the first section of this chapter, 'What school management staff need to know', the issues of how bullying behaviour is defined and the forms that bullying behaviour takes in schools were outlined. The 'no blame' philosophy and approach, as well as the notion of viewing bullying as a school community issue, were advocated.

- Some key issues for consideration were presented at the beginning of the second major section, 'Formulating effective anti-bullying policy in schools'. Consultation and collaboration with the school community was emphasized as an imperative. Guidance was also given around the dissemination, promotion, evaluation and review of the policy.

- The final major section of this chapter concerned itself with 'Formulating effective anti-bullying strategies in schools' – both countering strategies (including the reporting, investigation and recording of incidents of alleged bullying behaviour, and sanctions and support systems) and preventative strategies with students in the classroom.

FURTHER RESOURCES FOR SCHOOL MANAGEMENT STAFF

Elliot, M. (ed). (2002) *Bullying: A Practical Guide to Coping in Schools*. 3rd edition. London: Longman.

Olweus, D. (1993) *Bullying at School: What We Know and What We Can Do*. Oxford: Blackwell.

Rigby, K. (2001) *Stop the Bullying: A Handbook for Schools*. Australia: ACER.

Chapter 3

What teachers need to to know

> **━━━━━ WHAT'S IN THIS CHAPTER**
>
> This chapter has been written primarily for those involved in classroom work with students – whether they are teachers, resource teachers, classroom/teaching assistants, multi-agency staff or educational psychologists. For the sake of convenience, these people have been loosely termed 'classroom staff', and with such personnel in mind, the following items have been included in this chapter:
>
> ● What classroom staff need to know
>
> ● Dealing with incidents of bullying behaviour
>
> ● Preventative strategies: ideas for classroom activities
>
> ● A brief note on classroom staff and bullying behaviour in the workplace.

Note for trainers and school management staff

In Appendices C and D, there are copies of sets of model slides (in Microsoft PowerPoint format) that might be used in:

1 talks with parents / members of the general public in the school community (Appendix C)

2 general talks with school students (Appendix D).

The information on these sets of slides is based on a condensation of the key points of Chapters 4 and 5 respectively.

WHAT CLASSROOM STAFF NEED TO KNOW

Key issues in anti-bullying work

Important note to the reader: if you have begun reading at this chapter, please note that in order to save word space within this chapter, members of classroom staff are referred in the first instance to the previous chapter (Chapter 2), and very much urged to read the following sections: 'How bullying is defined, and the forms it takes'; 'The 'no blame' philosophy and approach'; and, 'Bullying behaviour as a school community issue'. Thereafter, he or she is encouraged to resume reading this chapter.

Anti-bullying policy in schools and the role of classroom staff in anti-bullying work

All anti-bullying efforts in schools – be they strategies and procedures for dealing with incidents of bullying behaviour, or for preventing further incidences, or support services for those involved in bullying behaviour – should be underpinned by an overall anti-bullying policy. This should be formulated by the responsible members within the school's management staff, in consultation with all groups within the school community – school management staff, classroom staff, non-teaching staff, students and parents of the school's students. The interested reader is very much advised to return to Chapter 2, where the majority of the chapter deals with anti-bullying policy formation and all of its attendant issues.

Put most simply, *the role of classroom staff in anti-bullying work is the practical and day-to-day implementation of the procedures and strategies specified in the school's anti-bullying policy.* At a conceptual level, it is possible to render distinct strategies for dealing with incidents of bullying behaviour (this section), and preventative strategies that can be taught/implemented through specific classroom activities (the next section in this chapter). Practically, all anti-bullying work makes certain skills and personal demands upon members of classroom staff. The purpose of this chapter is to help equip classroom staff with the skills and techniques that they need in order to be, and to feel, effective in making their contributions to the school's overall anti-bullying work.

More generally, even though teachers may not be universally recognized as 'shapers of young minds', they must be reckoned as having a very strong, if not profound, influence upon the attitudes and behaviour of young people in their care. For this reason, classroom staff have been encouraged consistently throughout this chapter to take every opportunity to convey an anti-bullying (and thereby anti-violence and pro-social) message to their students. One way in which this may be modelled is in how the classroom staff deal with situations of conflict between students; it is to this important issue that we shall now attend.

DEALING WITH INCIDENTS OF BULLYING BEHAVIOUR

Conflict resolution and conflict management

At the root of most of today's societal problems are sets of people who don't get along with each other. If one thinks, also at a societal level, of the long-standing international disputes in which so many people have suffered and died, and in some instances ended up charged with manslaughter or murder, one is forced to acknowledge that it is certainly not an easy task to resolve conflict. As an overall process, conflict resolution can be thought of in terms of a five stage model: (1) *identification* – of the person(s) who is/are a cause for concern; (2) *assessment* of the problem, that is, what the full nature of the conflict is; (3) *formulation* of the causes of the problem, that is, why it occurs; (4) *intervention* – finding ways to deal with the problem; and, (5) *evaluation* of the intervention.

In order to take one's part as a facilitator in conflict resolution, being (and, perhaps as importantly, being perceived to be) objective is essential. Involved parties will need to know that the facilitator will hear *everyone's* perspective, to which he or she will give equal and fair consideration, and that he or she will not make a decision or take action until he or she has heard everyone's perspective. It is likewise important to communicate that when action is taken, it will be fair and just, and a direct consequence of the choices made by the person or people in the situation of conflict, and in his or her subsequent behaviour.

Naturally, all of this must be conveyed before the attempt at conflict resolution, and through the facilitator's interactions with the aggrieved parties. Setting up ground rules can be helpful, particularly when working with very young people (that is, only one person speaking at a time – everyone shall get her or his turn, so no need for interruptions; no shouting, swearing, blasphemy; leave the past in the past, and so on). Obviously, everyone must agree to these ground rules at the start. Finally, if a facilitator wants to make a fair decision, and be perceived to be doing so, he or she must get all the facts, and perhaps be prepared to make notes in order to assist his or her doing so.

In conflict resolution, one must also be aware of the inherent emotional nature of what lies behind conflict situations: people rarely fight about facts or events, but rather, how they feel about them. This feelings content should be both acknowledged and managed; it is necessary to work constructively at the emotional level. To facilitate the expression of feelings, one should attend to the person's/people's safety needs; and employ the use of active listening and open-ended and feeling-level questions, taking an empathic standpoint throughout.

Where it is not possible to resolve a conflict – where no compromise is possible – then conflict management may be possible. For a genuine resolution of conflict, compromise is necessary. It may be that, for whatever reason, compromise is either impossible or will remain non-forthcoming for the foreseeable future, in which time the conflict is likely to either remain as destructive as ever or even to escalate. In this case, although there is no compromise between the two parties, they can enter into a voluntary agreement (arbitrated by a neutral third party acceptable to both sides) that binds them both to a set of rules or agreements designed to manage the causes and effects of the present conflict. Neither side has had to 'back down' or 'lose face'; the situation of conflict has been managed, and it is to be hoped that as a result of the management strategies that have been put in place that in the fullness of time compromise between the antagonists will become a possibility. In our own time, a societal example of a conflict management strategy has been the Good Friday Agreement in Northern Ireland. In the school situation, an example might be if two people have been persistently fighting one another and cannot put aside their differences, they can at least agree that their conflict is doing neither of them any good – rather, it is getting them both into trouble at school. Although it may be impossible for them to 'make friends', or even to feel neutral towards one another, they can involve themselves in a comprehensive plan to keep away from one another entirely, and be assisted in this planning process by a member of classroom or school management staff.

Although it is helpful to think of the possible resolution of many acts of aggressive behaviour in schools in terms of conflict resolution/conflict management, it should be noted that many incidents of bullying behaviour and harassment have very little to do with interpersonal conflict at all. Conflict usually involves at least two parties who are mutually antagonistic. The target of bullying behaviour or harassment may not, at least at the outset, have any strong feelings towards the perpetrator at all, let alone feels antagonistic towards him or her. In many cases, people are targeted, or singled out for bullying, not because of a mutual dislike between them and the perpetrator, but because of the perpetrator's desire to manipulate and exert power over others. This means that the processes by which one deals practically with bullying behaviour may be a little different from those used in dealing with other forms of aggressive behaviour.

Support strategies for those involved in bullying behaviour

The 'no blame' approach (see Chapter 2) informs us that both those involved in bullying behaviour as victims, and those involved as perpetrators, need the help and support of responsible adults within the school community. It is not enough simply to provide counselling services/emotional support for those who have been targeted – this is just one of a set of mediums of support that may be established. In many cases, social skills work may be an option. This is true for the anti-social persistent perpetrator, or indeed the so-called 'provocative victim' – in each case, the student concerned may have (and perhaps is unaware of) a personal interactive style that increases his or her propensity to be involved in situations of bullying behaviour. Such a person's awareness of how he or she relates to and interacts with others can be gently pointed out, and new social strategies can be suggested and taught by a classroom staff member with an appropriate pastoral role.

Finally, not everyone who is accused of bullying is aware that what he or she is doing is hurtful to others; or, the person may feel relatively out of control of how he or she emotionally responds in certain situations. Bullying is by definition a deliberate act, but sometimes a person may feel bullied (or at least harassed, aggressed or some form of hurt), regardless of whether the perpetrator intended this or not. The 'unintentional perpetrator' is limited by one or more of three things: a lack of self-awareness (of the nature or consequences of his or her actions), a lack of other-awareness (of how other people feel or are affected by his or her actions) or a lack of impulse control (he or she is unaware of his or her authority over and responsibility for his or her emotional responses – usually anger or excitement). In the case of the first two, social skills work might be usefully employed; in the case of the latter, some work on emotional management (and perhaps especially anger management) with a suitably qualified professional or skilled classroom staff member is probably the best strategy.

PREVENTATIVE STRATEGIES: IDEAS FOR CLASSROOM ACTIVITIES

General talks to class groups about bullying behaviour

Years ago, one of the authors remembers hearing about a school in England where in Assembly, the headteacher regularly addressed his students with the news that this was a 'telling school'. 'Not every school is a "telling school"', the headteacher would say, 'but this one is. This means that if anybody hurts us or otherwise picks on us, or persistently and deliberately leaves us out of things, or makes us feel bad in anyway, we tell a member of the school staff. And if we see anyone else being hurt, or picked on, or left out, or feeling bad, then we do what we can to help – by telling a member of school staff. That's what we mean by a "telling school".' He also encouraged them to tell if they were victimized out of school. The headteacher in question believed (rightly, we think) that this was diminishing the unwritten 'code of the playground' that 'ratting', 'snitching', 'clyping' – call it what you will – was a bad thing to do, and that the students under his care were more likely to report having been bullied. Very recently, the same author was organizing in-service teacher training at a school in Ireland, and the school principal informed the author that her school was a 'telling school'. News of good practice obviously spreads.

The key thing here seems to be that an anti-bullying message can very easily be given to students on a regular basis. In giving such general talks, repetition (as in so many aspects of general educational practise) seems to be essential. One would not, after all, expect a student to be able accurately to conjugate a French verb on the basis of one passive hearing, but instead encourage the student to repeat the conjugation of the verb for himself or herself, and to learn to use the various forms of the verb in meaningful sentence constructions.

The content of such talks should reflect how the school and the teachers conceive of bullying, such ideas being immediately underpinned by the school's code of anti-bullying policy and procedures (see section 'Anti-bullying policy in schools' above, and Chapter 2, section 'Formulating effective anti-bullying policy in schools'. Irrespective of the precise wording of individual school's policy statements, essential ideas to put across to young people will be: (1) what bullying is, and the different forms that it can take; (2) that bullying is seen in this school, as an unacceptable form of behaviour; (3) that we all have a responsibility to safeguard the well-being of others; (4) that if we are being bullied, or if we know about someone else being bullied, that the best way to get help is to tell a member of school staff; (5) that violent retaliation will only make things worse; and (6) that everyone has a right to a school that is free from bullying and harassment, and that we all have to play our part in achieving this.

These ideas, of course, should be put across to the students in words that they can understand. Different schools will have slightly different set-ups in terms of who has what might be called regular 'pastoral responsibility' for class groups; regardless of whether this is a principal/headteacher, year head or class teacher/tutor, an eminently achievable aim would be that every child in the school hears such a talk at least once a term. Readers will perhaps be interested to know that Chapter 5 of this book has been written for young people, and its corresponding appendix, Appendix D, comprises a sample 'PowerPoint' presentation, 'Resources for general talks with students'.

As well as simple repetition, if learning is to be of a meaningful and long-lasting nature, the students' active involvement within the learning process must be fostered. It is to such techniques that we shall now attend in the sections that follow.

Specific anti-bullying activity classes

Whole-class groups with a self-esteem focus

It is desirable and practical to conduct anti-bullying work with class groups as a whole. As the content of anti-bullying sessions is rather less focused around a knowledge base than an attitudinal/emotional base – in other words, personal learning – *the emotional needs of the students must be constantly kept in mind.* A person learns most effectively when his or her self-esteem needs are met. On a practical level, this means that the goal should be that every child – regardless of age or ability level – can participate fully in the class's anti-bullying activities. The practical challenges of achieving this goal can be tough to overcome, but the goal should always be aimed at.

Methodologically, anti-bullying sessions may be structured around a combination of stimulating (awareness-raising) and creative media (that is, non-pen-and-paper tasks) and facilitator-led, structured discussion work. For the facilitator, this means that careful planning of anti-bullying activity sessions is necessary. We suggest creative media, rather than pen-and-paper tasks, for three reasons. First, very young children have not yet accrued the writing skills to express themselves. Secondly, with our self-esteem focus in mind, academically less gifted pupils may have come to dread or reject written tasks in general as something they are 'weak' at, and an exercise in which they feel 'less than' their fellow students and bad about themselves. Finally, the use of creative media in a class marks the anti-bullying activity session as something different from the norm, something fun and enjoyable, where they (hopefully) learn something of personal value.

It is, of course, advisable to use a combination of creative media in anti-bullying work, perhaps in the course of a series of sessions. After all, not every student either enjoys or can learn from the same activity. The important thing is to avoid the creative work taking over, or becoming at all competitive – what matters is that everyone is joining in. For this reason, a facilitator might like to choose a medium that he or she is fairly or completely inept in – this sends a strong message that it is the taking part that counts. Of course, the real learning for the students is in the discussion aspects of the session. This involves group work, either small or whole class, or a combination of the two, and undertaking this sort of work brings up a number of important issues that are discussed below.

Group work and group boundaries

Some teachers are fully familiar with, and regularly use, 'circle time' and group work in their everyday teaching practise. Some students experience and contribute to group discussions every day in class time at school. On the other hand, some teachers prefer to teach solely curriculum-based academic material from the front of the class to students who sit quietly and passively in rows, and some students may not have sat in a circle with a class teacher since they were last read a fairy story. In the latter case, the sort of group discussion work that is advocated in most of the anti-bullying activities that follow is likely to be a challenge for both the teacher and the students.

First, the teacher must be prepared to make a mental shift from 'instructor' to 'facilitator'. Whilst the overall content of the class is determined by the school staff, the specifics will be pupil led. This will be liberating for the students, but initially potentially challenging for the teacher. His or her sense of liberation will come as soon as he or she is comfortable in teaching in this type of set-up. The teacher should also acknowledge to the students that this is a new and different classroom teaching situation, but one which is particularly appropriate for the material that the class is to deal with. The 'horses for courses' argument is helpful – after all, one goes to a language laboratory (or similarly equipped room) to learn French or German, and one would not expect to learn soccer, rugby or hockey skills is the art room!

It is also noteworthy that the sense of safety that both students and teachers need in approaching a group discussion session may be reinforced by a set of 'class rules'. This in itself may be a helpful exercise; if it is formalized, it can be undertaken as a 'class charter' activity (see Action suggestion 3.4, below). Obviously, the school rules still apply! However, the facilitator might well pose the question: given the fact that as a class people will be, to a certain extent, discussing feelings, what extra rules do we need, and can we agree upon? Mutual respect and privacy will naturally be concerns. The explicit goal will be that *everyone feels safe and happy enough to contribute what he or she can to the discussion*. Finally, given the slim but nonetheless possible potential for emotional 'fallout' from the session, discussion work has a debriefing function. Even though the discussion exercises are student driven and facilitator led, bullying is an emotive issue (certainly so for those who are currently victim to it). This could give rise to some students becoming upset or distressed. *It is strongly advised that before beginning this sort of classroom activity that a link with pastoral or student care services within the school should be established.*

Action suggestion 3.1: ideas for warm-up activities

People   You (trainer/member of classroom staff), student class group

Materials   None

Methods   Many 'warm-up' games and activities will already be familiar to classroom staff. There are numerous verbal games that may be used to help members of a newly formed group to remember each other's names; there are the traditional mobility games often used in primary school physical education; there are also games that rely on memory and general/popular knowledge. In the situation of 'warming-up' a class group for anti-bullying work, one thing is perhaps most important – achieving a pro-social atmosphere. The following activities can help in this:

1 *A mobility game.* Very simply, the students walk around the room (avoiding charging into one another and items of classroom furniture). Whenever the facilitator signals them to stop (say, by clapping his or her hands), the students stop and shake hands with the nearest person to them. Trying to shake hands with three people at once is a lot of fun for younger children.

2 *An 'introduce yourself' game.* The facilitator explains to the class that everybody is good at a number of things. People can be good at a game, sport or hobby; they can be good at a certain subject at school; they can be a good brother or sister, son or daughter, grandson or

CONTINUED

granddaughter; they could be good at talking, or good at listening. The list is endless (and should appear so to the students). Each student then in turn has to stand up, and introduce himself or herself according to the following formula: 'My name is (insert name) and one of the things I'm good at is ... .' The facilitator might either start or end things by introducing himself or herself according to the same formula, saying what he or she is good at. This could be something serious, that the students know about: 'My name is Mrs Smith and one of the things I'm good at is teaching people how to speak French.' Or, if the facilitator feels the need to humanize himself or herself a little, it could be something trivial, that the students don't know about: 'My name is Mr Jones, and one of the things I'm good at is cooking omelettes.' A little bit of humour is often a nice touch, but the humour should never be self-deprecating. Hence, 'My name is Darren, and one of the things I'm good at is messing about' is probably fine, but 'My name is Simon and I'm not good at anything' is certainly not. Facilitators should gently help a student to think of something that he or she is good at for himself or herself rather than making direct suggestions, and limit the amount of suggestions made to others from 'the floor'.

3 *Identifying things you like about others.* Students stand facing each other in two lines. In silence (don't laugh!), they look at the person standing opposite them. They are then told to think about (at least) one thing that they like about the other person. They will not have to say this out loud, or even to the other person. They just have to think about one thing, no matter how small, that they like about the person opposite to them. After all, you don't have to be a person's friend, or to know them particularly well, in order to find just one small thing that you like about them. After a few moments, the activity stops. The students are told that they can tell the other person what they liked about them at another time if they want to.

Action suggestion 3.2: a sample video/discussion session

People   You (trainer/member of classroom staff), student class group

Materials   Age-appropriate video extract of approximately ten minutes in length; video recorder and television; board or flip chart for recording students' suggestions and reactions; writing materials for students

Methods   This is a good session to be used in awareness-raising phase of a class's anti-bullying work, hence, quite early on in the overall process. The exercise is methodologically simple; essentially, the students watch part of a film, and engage in a structured discussion about it. However, the rationale behind the phases of this type of exercise will be explained further.

1 *Pre-classroom phase/preparation*. An essential aspect is, of course, the selection of the video extract. There are many films that portray acts of bullying and violence – some more responsibly than others – and this is indeed an important consideration. The extract should be one which young people can relate to; one which involves young people of about their own age; and one that is realistic and relevant, without being potentially shocking or traumatizing (video certification should be checked in the first instance). The extract should be about 10 minutes long in duration. This is enough to stimulate discussion; it is unnecessary (and perhaps unrealistic) to watch an entire film with a view to discussing one or two key scenes. Finally, in terms of continuation, the extract itself should be viewable in itself without too much explanation being necessary in order for students to understand the narrative. The part of this phase is to prepare questions and discussion points for the class work that is to follow the viewing of the film extract (see paragraphs 3 and 4 below).

2 *Watching the film extract*. An extract that has been used by one of the authors in work with older teenagers (the certification of this film is 15) runs something like this: there are four key characters – a 'victim' ('Chris', 12 years old), a 'victim's friend' ('Jordie', also 12 years old), a 'bully' ('Ace', about 18 years old), and a 'bully's friend' ('Eyeball', also about 18 years old). In the first scene, we find out that Jordie's brother died the previous year, but before he did so, gave Jordie his baseball cap. Hence, this cap means quite a lot to him. The next scene is a comical one, in which Jordie meets up with his friend Chris, and they pull off a boyhood prank.

The final scene in the extract is the one in which the 'bullying' takes place. Jordie and Chris run into the 'bully' of the piece, Ace, and his

CONTINUED

accomplice, Eyeball. Here we find out that as well as being the bully's (Ace's) friend, he is also, in his person, the victim's (Chris's) brother. Initially, Ace takes Jordie's baseball cap from him. When Chris tries to get the baseball cap back for Jordie, Ace turns his aggression onto Chris, forcing him to apologise for insulting him by pinning him to the floor, and holding a lit cigarette close to his eye. Eyeball joins in the persecution in two ways; first, he consistently insults both Chris and Jordie; secondly, he does absolutely nothing at all to protect the 'victim' of the piece, his brother, Chris.

After such an extract, the class can then be usefully engaged in a structured discussion.

3 *Thinking about the film extract.* Some thought needs to go into preparing some questions for discussion. It is best done in a 'circle-time' type of set-up, and the discussion can include some small-group work if the students are able and keen on this type of activity. In the example given above, the class group was divided into four subgroups, and each group had to take one of the characters. Each subgroup elected a 'scribe' (to write down the comments on behalf of the group) and a 'spokesperson' (someone to convey their group member's comments, that is, an elaboration of what the 'scribe' had written down) to the rest of the class. (Even assisting the groups in the democratic 'election' of people to these roles, rather than relying upon the 'press-ganging' that might occur, is a pro-social exercise in itself.) Some questions might be:

(a) What role did your group's character play in the bullying situation (i.e. victim, victim's friend, bully, bully's friend)?

(b) How old was your group's character?

(c) Did you like your group's character? If so, why? If not, why not?

(d) What did your group's character do in the bullying situation?

(e) Do you think he/she did the right thing? If so, why? If not, why not?

(f) What could he/she have done differently? Why?

(g) What would you have (liked to) have done if you were in your character's place in that situation?

4 *Whole-class discussion*. First, in a situation where subgroups have been used, each group's spokesperson tells the rest of the class the ideas they have had. The other groups listen whilst this is going on, and may be asked to volunteer their contributions and reactions to the aspect of the film that the spokesperson is addressing. Each group takes its turn. Finally, the class as a whole, in a facilitated open discussion, can respond to further questions:

(a) Which character did we like best, and why?

(b) Which character did we like least, and why?

(c) Do incidents like the one we saw in the film ever happen?

(d) What could/should we do in such a situation, and why?

(e) What have we learnt from today's class?

Note: Readers may be interested to know, and perhaps could predict, that in the extract we have described, the least popular character was invariably (regardless of the age or gender of the students) Eyeball, the 'bully's friend' and the 'victim's' brother. Why? One reason is that he was a bully himself – although he didn't physically assault anyone, he still insulted them (which was identified as a type of bullying). Both Ace and Eyeball were generally disliked because their bullying was seen as totally unfair, due to the age difference – here were 18-year-old young men picking on 12-year-old boys. However, the aspect that was most forcibly argued by the students was the feeling that Eyeball should have stood up for his brother (Chris). In other words, he should have gone against his own friend (Ace) and stopped the bullying. A case of 'blood being thicker than water'? Probably. But this finding also shows that at a level, every child/teenager knows that the actions of a bully are unfair; and also, that people have a responsibility to stop bullying (even if this pro-social action only extends to blood relations, it could still be built upon, and into a general principle). Naturally, the difficulty of going against one's friends – withstanding the peer pressure to join in bullying – was acknowledged, but the very fact that the students argued spontaneously and vigorously that this should have been done, at least in this case, was encouraging.

Visual arts: posters, pictures and sculpture

Many young people like to draw and paint. Given the timing of the information technology revolution, others have the computer skills to produce posters, flyers and documents of an extremely professional quality. The visual arts provide possibly the most simple and yet effective way of harnessing young people's creative abilities into constructing their own anti-bullying message. Even the youngest child, incapable of printing language, can (by school age) draw pictures of (say) what bullies are like, providing an often astonishingly profound insight into that child's understanding by adults who spend any time looking at such work. Older children (late primary age and above) and teenagers can use their experience of the world, in particular its popular media and advertising, to construct posters that convey an anti-bullying message. Finally, even emotionally sophisticated teenagers (and adult facilitators, too) can re-experience the joys of more innocent years when deliciously messy sculpture sessions are involved. Air-drying clay, plaster of Paris, chicken wire (for more elaborate construction work), what appears to be household waste (empty bottles and canisters), as well as adornments such as paint, textiles, feathers, seashells, are all readily and cheaply available, and ideal for sculpture work. An example of such a session is given in 'Action suggestion 3.3'.

Action suggestion 3.3: a sample crafts/discussion session

People   You (trainer/member of classroom staff), student class group

Materials   Refuse sacks, tape, a collection of empty bottles and containers, air-drying clay, various textiles (rags, material, coloured paper or cardboard, felt), poster paints, scissors, glue, items for decoration (for example, sea shells, bottle tops, drinking straws, pipe cleaners, feathers, leaves, silk flowers, and so on). In another part of the room, enough chairs for everyone set up in a circle.

Methods   This is an example of a sculpture/discussion session that can be used with older primary and secondary school age students. It is best done after the students have already done some awareness-raising work and discussion about bullying behaviour.

1 *Before the session.* The students should be told beforehand that they will be doing some art work at this time, and that they will need to protect their clothes – so they should bring in an apron or overall, or a man's shirt. (It is advisable for the facilitator to bring in a few of these, as there are always some students who will forget). Immediately before the session, the room should be reorganized; anything that is likely to

be damaged by paint, glue or clay should be put away (use an uncarpeted room), and desks should be covered. A cheap and easy way of covering desks is to split large refuse sacks into plastic sheets, and then to tape these over the desk tops so that they do not move.

2 *Setting up and doing the sculpture task.* The students walk into this rather odd environment and told a bit about what sculpture is. They are then reminded of the work they have already done on bullying. They are told what they are doing – making bottle sculptures. They can make a bottle into anything they like, and they can decorate the bottle in any way that they like (they will have air-drying clay, textiles, poster paints, scissors, glue, and any items for decoration that the facilitator can get hold of (see suggestions above in 'Materials'). The first major rule is this – the sculpture must say something about the work we have done on stopping bullying behaviour. Bottles are, of course, a rather ubiquitous shape; as a basis for a sculpture, a young child might use it as the body of a 'bully' figurine. *Please note that students should be discouraged from sculpting stereotypical 'victim' figures, that is, 'geeks', 'losers' or 'wimps'.* This would give the message that some people 'deserve' to be bullied, which entirely undermines the whole ethos of anti-bullying work. Older students can deal with more abstract notions; a bottle can serve as the base of an erupting volcano, for example, symbolizing the pent-up and explosively released angry emotions that we experience when we have been victimized.

3 *Discussing the task.* The second major rule of this session is that when the facilitator signals them to stop – which he or she will do so every 15 minutes or so – that they must come into the circle, and discuss how they are getting on with their sculptures. The facilitator should try to put interesting questions to the group, and thus foster a whole class discussion: is the task an easy one? Is it harder than you thought? What is it like trying to express your thoughts and feelings through working with sculpture? Has doing this helped you to think about bullying behaviour and anti-bullying work in a different way at all? How do you feel about putting your work on display?

4 *Display.* Bottle sculptures are often very attractive, and because of their size, can very easily be put on display. Of course, if a student really doesn't want to put his or her work on display, his or her feelings should be respected.

Performance arts: music, drama, film script and role-play

Musical composition is immensely popular with some students. Writing in 2004, with rap as perhaps the most popular musical medium amongst secondary students, equipment is hence very much simplified – essentially, all that is needed is a drum machine (and someone's ability to use/programme it) or human-based percussion (many young people can provide a 'human beat-box' vocally). Some teachers recoil at the idea of rap, shocked (perhaps justifiably so) by the explicit misogyny and glorification of street violence portrayed in some of the 'gangsta' rap styles. However, to write off an entire medium is possibly too drastic a step. Firstly, one of the reasons for the continued commercial success of the artist Eminem is his willingness to explore a diversity of themes within his own medium. Rap needn't be about glorifying violence, anymore than some parents in the 1950s assumed all rock 'n' roll music glorified sexual immorality. Secondly, one should remember that the emotional passion of rap is due to that it is, properly considered, the 'folk'/street music of an oppressed people – and what the anger inherent in rap is principally derived from is the experience of social injustice and inequality. If we focus on lyrical content – as it will necessarily be focused in an anti-bullying work situation – then rap is an accessible and immediately relevant medium in which students truly can be self-directive and motivated in their work. Naturally, other musical mediums are available for young people who are enthusiastic about other musical genres, and for younger children. Some of these will depend upon the students'/teacher's ability to play an instrument sufficiently well to permit composition – but writing lyrics in the form of poetry, and thinking of simple vocal melodies and/or harmonies, is sufficiently simple for even the youngest and those who regard themselves as 'not musical' to master.

Some teachers are very much aware of the possibilities of drama, film and role-play in helping to raise students' awareness of various issues. However, there is a possibility of retraumatizing students who have been bullied in a role-play situation. As this is a cause for concern the authors, in their work as in-service training providers, have not seen fit to generally recommend such a methodology. After all, in a role-play situation, or an original dramatic composition, the content of what is played out is relatively 'out of the control' of classroom staff and therefore, as a facilitator, one cannot have any real confidence in the 'staged' victimization of a student 'actor' being entirely fictional. Yet drama is a powerful and potentially extremely instructive medium. Some plays with an anti-bullying content are available for classroom/school use (see 'useful resources' at the end of this book); it may also be possible to stage an original play in school, providing that classroom staff have a good level of influence over at least the editing of the scripts. In terms of the rather more spontaneous, more inclusive and less formal use of class role-play activities, for the reasons outlined above, we believe that these are of some use in exploring key issues around bullying behaviour, rather than addressing bullying behaviour directly. Areas such as peer pressure, dynamics of friendships and 'dealing with feelings' are all potentially useful themes to introduce in the course of conducting anti-bullying work, and themes that lend themselves to students' immediate knowledge and experience, whilst remaining relatively 'safe' for classroom use. Developing a film script may also provide students with an exciting, rich and engaging means of identifying with and understanding the problems of bullying and victimisation.

Action suggestion 3.4: the use of class charters

People   You (trainer/member of classroom staff), student class group

Materials   Nothing other than standard classroom stationery

Methods   A class charter is an excellent document to work towards in a class's/school's anti-bullying work. Before this type of exercise, the students awareness of bullying as an issue to be tackled will have been raised (perhaps through the general efforts of the school, or the types of exercises already mentioned in the first three 'action suggestions' of this chapter. The process of constructing a charter is rather simple, but perhaps deserves some commentary:

1   The students are asked to imagine that they are in charge of the class/year group/school, and to put themselves in the position of the class teacher/year head/principal. What rules would they make against bullying? With students from the middle primary years upwards, it can help to put the students into pairs, or small (three to four members) discussion groups in order to generate ideas (upon which they should all achieve consensus) which they can then write down, perhaps on some pre-prepared answer sheets. Younger students can call out their answers, which can be written on the board by the facilitator. Naturally, the facilitator should, in this situation, encourage as many suggestions as possible – every single student should be involved.

It is, of course, important to set some boundaries. Hopefully, through previous awareness-raising anti-bullying work, students will have been familiarized with the idea that violent retaliation is not an option. Violence only breeds more violence. This needs to be explained in a language that the students understand – students must see the bankruptcy of any form of 'self-policing' through the organization of gangs, posses or other forms of vigilante action for themselves. If I get my brother to beat up the person who bullied me, then the bully brings the rest of his or her family to beat up me and my brother – then I get all of my friends and family to beat up the bully and his or her family – then he or she brings half of the neighbourhood ... and then, sooner or later, someone or all of us ends up expelled from school/seriously

CONTINUED

injured/facing criminal charges. It is possible that there is a local situation that the students in an area may know about that can be brought to mind in order to illustrate this point.

In a class where students are rather less than eager to comply with teachers'/school's initiatives, a charter can be an effective way of working. In a class where a 'siege' mentality exists – the 'us against them' mentality ('them' being parents, teachers, any authority figure), this can be used to the good provided a general condemnation of the unfairness of bullying behaviour can be agreed upon. Instead of being asked, 'what rules could we make against bullying?', such a class could be addressed thus: 'Can you as a class find some ways to look out for each other and prevent anybody in this room from being bullied?'

2   The facilitator should then take charge of getting all of the students' suggestions into the general shape of a charter. A content analysis should then be made. The tactic should not be to pick what the facilitator considers to be 'the best', or even the most frequent rules, although this second point is of course important. The idea is to get the totality of the students' suggestions into a workable format, say, eight to ten short statements. It is preferable to keep the students' own language as far as is possible. It is to be expected that students will have made suggestions around both the prevention and countering of bullying behaviour, so very little 'editing' will be required – only, perhaps, the editing out of suggestions that are blatantly out of keeping with anti-bullying ethos. In the case of the younger class, who have not written suggestions for themselves, the statements transcribed from them by the facilitator on the board can be worked through in a facilitated whole class discussion, and a final set of suggestions agreed upon.

3   This phase is an important one – the public display of the final version of the charter. If the artistic execution abilities of the facilitator far exceed those of his or her class, then the facilitator may decide to 'type up' the final version. Certainly, the final version will need to be enlarged to poster size and laminated. The charter can then be put on display in the class's home or base room.

4   If the charter is, as we would suggest, to be used 'for real' in the class/school – the students' input here gives them a very real positive influence over how bullying behaviour is countered and prevented. The construction of such a charter (or set of charters, working systematically through each class) provides an ideal opportunity to integrate students' perspectives into the school's anti-bullying policy and practise (see Chapter 2 in general, and Action suggestion 2.5 in particular).

CONTINUED

Depending on the students' age/level of understanding, this information can be fed back to the students. The overall idea, as with any charter is to give the people whom the charter is designed to serve a sense of ownership over the process. And as one child responded when one of the authors asked her if she thought she and her classmates would follow the charter that they had just completed work upon, 'You'd have to be an awful idiot to break your own rules'.

Finally, as was indicated in Chaper 2 (see 'Action suggestion 2.5'), the public display of students' own contributions to the anti-bullying work of a school is immensely important. Holding an 'anti-bullying week', or 'anti-bullying day', to which parents and members of the local community are invited, gives a chance for schools and their students to show off their good work. Even if holding such an event is, for whatever reason, not an option, the students' work should be displayed as publicly as possible. Don't let a students' anti-bullying poster turn yellow in a drawer; don't let their music go unheard; don't let their performances go unseen. The opportunity to enhance students' self-esteem by a publc acknowledgement of the contributions they have made is simply too good to miss.

Anti-bullying across the curriculum

When a strong anti-bullying ethos is genuinely embedded into the fabric of the school, classroom staff can feel confident in using their own ingenuity in conveying an 'anti-bullying' message through their general teaching practice, where such a thing is feasible. As primary-level teachers have perhaps more freedom over the structuring of their own class's learning than do secondary level teachers, they may more readily find such opportunities. Having said this, it is possible to approach the issue of anti-bullying through secondary teaching practise, as our notes immediately below will help us illustrate.

Because of the enormous amount of written material that has been produced in the English language, teachers of English probably have the simplest means of introducing anti-bullying content into their everyday teaching practise. Where syllabi and curricula are not too overprescriptive, English teachers can almost as easily use books and plays with a content that enables them to encourage students to think about issues of non-violence and equality as other types of publications. Naturally, a good deal of written literature in the English language reflects the preoccupations of the English-speaking world, one of which has always been aggressive behaviour. It is to be hoped that the list of useful resources at the end of this book will provide some useful suggestions; readers should also note that a fairly lengthy list of books written specifically for young people that address issues of bullying and violence has been included in the source list. We are fairly certain that English teachers will be able readily to identify other sources beyond those which we have provided – sections of Shakespeare's tragedies, for example, often illustrate the bankruptcy of violence and 'dirty tricks' campaigns.

In other commonly taught secondary school subjects, it is to be remembered that what young people most often find objectionable about bullying behaviour is its inherent unfairness – the tyranny of the aggressor over those who are, for whatever reason, not in a position to defend themselves. (Even the youngest child will agree that the bigger/older child who picks on the smaller/younger child is almost certainly in the wrong.) Sadly, the history of our species on this planet provides us with consistent and regular examples of tyranny and persecution in every time period. Therefore, teachers of what might be loosely termed the 'humanities' – history, religious education (and even human aspects of geography and economics) have many 'cues' at their disposal for helping students to think about the undesirability of bullying and victimization in a broader context. After all, is it even possible to talk about colonial history, or the history of the world wars of the twentieth century, without conveying such a message? Can an issue such as Third-World debt be explained to idealistically minded teenagers with the same cynicism that the political leaders of the western powerhouse economy states exhibit?

Other subjects taught at the secondary school level are perhaps less obvious in terms of how they lend themselves to the inclusion of an anti-bullying content. Still, two key principles remain; first, that classroom staff should take every opportunity to convey an anti-bullying message; secondly, that the inherent creativity and ingenuity of such personnel will provide the best means (and certainly, a more definite methodology than could possibly be provided in these rough guidelines) by which this may be concretely achieved. Teachers of modern languages, perhaps, if their curricula provide for the inclusion of aspects of cultural studies pertinent to the language, can find a similar way to those who teach the humanities into such a discussion. Both the past and the present of countries where the commonly taught modern languages are spoken provide numerous examples of injustice and violence. Even in the sciences, the consideration of human implications for scientific achievements – and even, at an advanced level, the rather cut-throat world of scientific research – provide a natural way in which a discussion around ethics and values clarification can be introduced. The discussion of health and safety issues in the practical/vocational subjects can at least be used to encourage students to think pro-socially and around their collective responsibility for the well-being of others. Even in mathematics, classes can provide for the application of statistical analyses to data accrued from class or school surveys of bullying.

A BRIEF NOTE ON CLASSROOM STAFF AND BULLYING BEHAVIOUR IN THE WORKPLACE

Classroom staff and bullying behaviour

If social scientists may be considered to have drawn our general (and our popular media's) attention to the reality of the problems of bullying amongst school students over the last 30 or so years, then their research colleagues must also be reckoned to have drawn attention in a similar way, over the last decade or two, to the reality of bullying within the workplace. If workplace bullying exists (as workplace bullying researchers have shown us) in the full spectrum of occupational environments, there is no convincing argument that springs to mind as to why we should expect the school as a workplace to be an exception to this.

Throughout this book, we have maintained both a 'no blame' approach (including the idea that anyone can be affected by or involved in bullying behaviour) and a 'whole-school' or 'community' approach (although our concern has been almost entirely focused upon the bullying behaviour that takes place between school students, this approach must by necessity allow for the acknowledgement that different groups within the school community can be affected by or involved in bullying behaviour). As we hold these approaches to be both meaningful and relevant, it is again only logically consistent to expect that at least some people who work within school systems to be involved in bullying behaviour as either perpetrators or victims.

Direction towards further resources

Sadly, there is only so much that can be covered in one book. Space does not permit us to consider the issue of workplace bullying in schools in any detail here; and to provide merely a cursory overview seems to us to be a profound disservice, given the serious effects that the experience of being bullied in the workplace can have. Rather than do this, we have elected to present an additional list of references (see the final section of the 'Useful resources' chapter of this book) where workplace bullying in general is covered in considerable, and what we hope to be helpful, detail.

SUMMARY

● In the first major section of this chapter, entitled 'What classroom staff need to know', cross-referencing was first made to key material covered in Chapter 2. There was then a consideration of the implications for classroom staff of anti-bullying policy in schools and the skills and techniques that staff need in conducting anti-bullying work.

● The second major section, 'Dealing with incidents of bullying behaviour', covered conflict resolution and conflict management, and support strategies for those involved in bullying behaviour, including emotional (anger) management work.

● The third and largest section, 'Preventative strategies: ideas for classroom activities', included notes on the use and content of general talks to class groups about bullying behaviour and a lengthy subsection on specific anti-bullying activity classes.

● The final section of this chapter was devoted to 'A brief note on classroom staff and bullying behaviour in the workplace'.

FURTHER RESOURCES FOR CLASSROOM STAFF

Elliot, M. and Shenton, G. (1999) *Bully-free: Activities to Promote Confidence and Friendship*. London: Kidscape.

Glover, D., Cartwright, N. and Gleeson, D. (1998) *Towards Bully-free Schools: Interventions in Action*. Buckingham: Open University Press.

Sullivan, K., Cleary, M. and Sullivan, G. (2004) *Bullying in Secondary Schools: What It Looks Like and How to Manage It*. London: Paul Chapman Publishing and Corwin Press.

Chapter 4

What parents need to know

Note for trainers and school management staff

In Appendix C, there is a copy of a set of model slides (in Microsoft PowerPoint format) that might be used at a parents' group presentation in school. The information on these slides is based on a condensation of the key points of this chapter.

WHAT PARENTS NEED TO KNOW

The different types of bullying

Bullying is a form of aggressive behaviour that is conducted by a person or group of people, on a systematic and ongoing basis, against a person who is singled out, and is relatively unable to defend himself or herself. It is not bullying, for instance, when people of around the same age and level of physical/social power have the occasional fight or quarrel. Although we have specified the 'systematic and ongoing' aspects of bullying, it should be noted that a one-off threat or incident that is unjustified and serves to intimidate on an ongoing basis may also be described as bullying. Traditionally, people have thought most often about physical assaults and intimidation when the word 'bullying' is mentioned. However, this only covers a small amount of the bullying that goes on in schools.

Verbal bullying is persistent name-calling, or 'slagging' (which hurts, insults or humiliates), or using a person consistently as a butt of jokes. If such verbal harassment is regularly and persistently directed at someone's family, ethnicity or religion, or couched in sexual innuendo, it is particularly likely to be experienced as bullying. Physical bullying is pushing, shoving, kicking, poking, tripping up, punching or striking with weapons or objects. This includes all forms of assaults, or the threats of physical assaults. Physical bullying may also take the form of causing deliberate damage to a person's clothes or personal property. Gesture bullying can include threatening non-verbal gestures, such as glances that convey messages of threat and intimidation. Extortion is the deliberate extraction of money, possessions or lunch vouchers, accompanied by threats. Victims of extortion may also be forced to commit anti-social acts, for example, theft or the vandalism of property. E-bullying is the sending of threatening or abusive material via electronic mail or text messages.

There are also many types of so-called 'indirect bullying' (distinguished from the more 'direct' or relatively 'open' attacks mentioned in the paragraph above). These can include socially isolating or ignoring someone, or attempting to make others dislike someone; the deliberate manipulation of friendship groups to make someone unpopular; the spreading of malicious rumours, falsehoods or gossip; the circulation of nasty notes or nasty pictures; and, the writing of insulting graffiti.

Researchers have found that males and females of school age tend to be involved to differing extents in the various types of bullying behaviour.[1] Very broadly speaking, boys are more likely than girls to physically bully their victims, whereas female perpetrators tend to favour the 'indirect' methods. As physical bullying is often more obvious (physical assaults tend to come to the attention of school authorities more quickly), and leaves physical evidence (in terms of cuts and bruises on the victim's body), than is 'indirect' bullying, the latter may go undetected for longer periods of time. Parents of daughters may, therefore, wish to take note of this point.

In this chapter, we have tried, in so far as it is possible, to talk about children/teenagers/young people who bully others/are engaged in bullying behaviour, rather than simply to refer to 'bullies'. Labelling someone as a 'bully' is not helpful; neither is attempting to seek out and punish people, which might be conceived of as the 'traditional' (and, notably, inherently flawed and usually unsuccessful) 'blame/punishment' approach. We advocate challenging and changing inappropriate behaviour – that is to say, teaching new skills, promoting understanding and resolving conflict. *Every person is capable of changing his or her behaviour*; indeed, our modern-day legal system is supposed to be based (at least partially) on rehabilitation of offenders, rather than the early medieval system of the exacting of vengeance. It is absolutely vital to note that young people who are involved in bullying, aggressive behaviour and harassment, either as victims or perpetrators (or in some cases, both), need the help and intervention of parents and school personnel. We have attempted to reflect this idea in the construction and material of this chapter.

Why parents are so important

Every responsible parent is concerned for the protection, safety and well-being of his or her child; and, along with school personnel, parents have a responsibility to ensure that their children/teenagers are not involved in inappropriate behaviours such as bullying or harassing other school students. Hence, in terms of efforts to be made to counter bullying, aggressive behaviour and harassment in schools, parents have an absolutely key role.

Quite naturally, and despite the protestations of some teenagers to the contrary, one's parents are generally the biggest single influence on one's attitudes and behaviour. Young people's attitudes towards aggression are often down to what they have seen in the home, as well as at school and in the peer group. Hence, we have included a section on how parents can act as positive role models *vis-à-vis* aggression later in this chapter (that is, in the section, 'What to do if your child/teenager is bullying others' below). We also believe that good communication between the home and the school is essential. For this reason, we have devoted an entire section of this chapter to 'Working with your child's/teenager's school against bullying' (see below).

Research shows that bullied young people are more likely to report having been bullied to their parents rather than to staff at their school.[2] However, for reasons such as the fear that the situation will become worse if one 'tells', many young people who are bullied are extraordinarily reluctant to report that they have been bullied to anyone at all. This often leaves the concerned parent in the dark as to whether his or her child/teenager has indeed been victimized. It also means that parents often have to do some 'detective work'. In order to assist parents, we have specified a list of 'signs and symptoms' of being bullied immediately below.

Signs and symptoms of being bullied

The following factors can be considered as indicative that a young person may be being bullied:

- *The young person looks distressed or anxious, and yet refuses to say what is wrong.* Remember, bullying is often surrounded by secrecy; and that the person who is bullying may threaten to make her or his attacks more severe, should the person being bullied say anything.

- *Unexplained cuts and bruises.* Some young people play contact sports, and (especially in young boys) some play can be of the 'rough and tumble' variety. However, physical evidence of punches and kicks to the face, head and body should never be ignored.

- *Damage to clothes, books, and school equipment.* This can be indicative of physical bullying; some people also perpetrate bullying through deliberate destruction or theft of their victim's possessions.

- *Doing worse at school than before.* A person's ability to concentrate, and his or her level of self-esteem, is very much connected to how well he or she works in the classroom and at home, and therefore the level of academic success he or she is likely to achieve. A sudden 'dip' in a child's academic attainment is often indicative of some problem, be that bullying or something else, and should be investigated.

- *Requests for extra money.* Some young people are bullied by demands for money, possessions, or even lunch vouchers. A person who bullies may also force his or her victim to steal (say, from shops or even houses) for him or her; this gives the person who bullies not only the money or possessions that have been stolen, but also an extra psychological 'hold' over the person being bullied.

- *Reluctance to go to school.* Obviously, a person who is being bullied may be reluctant to face the person or people who bully him or her. Some young people are, of course, less enthusiastic about school than others, so a sudden reluctance or increase in reluctance to go to school is a more accurate marker. Some school students are bullied on their way to or from school; hence, a new pattern of 'lateness' is also something to watch out for, particularly if this is associated with taking a 'new' route to school. For example, a child may choose to walk to school, rather than to take the bus (critically, upon which he or she is bullied) as he or she normally does, even though an outcome of this choice may be that he or she arrives late.

- *Changes in mood and behaviour.* This in itself can be difficult to establish, particularly in the teenage years, when an adolescent's social world is expanding rapidly, and his or her daily behaviour is increasingly influenced by his or her peers. However, a persistently low general mood may be a cause for parental concern, whether its cause is the experience of being bullied or some other factor.

- *Lower confidence and self-esteem.* Considerable evidence exists to show that there is a link between a person's level of self-esteem and his or her likelihood of being involved in bullying behaviour (see below). Low self-esteem is likely to manifest itself in a child's level of (particularly social) confidence, his or her lack of enthusiasm to try (particularly new) things, and a general appearance of either reservation and withdrawal, or of 'bluffing' one's way through. Naturally, some young people are by temperament quieter and more reserved than others; however, a sudden loss of self-esteem is often a sign that the young person has experienced or is experiencing a stressful situation, and hence should be investigated.

- *Complaints of headaches and stomach aches.* These can be real or imagined. If feigned, this is because a common physical symptom such as an unspecified 'pain' might get the person out of going to school (and thus facing his or her tormentors) for a day, but is unlikely to warrant further investigation (that is, a visit to the family doctor). However, these general aches may well be real; as many people are aware, chronic (that is to say, long-term) psychological stress leads to certain psychosomatic problems such as headaches and stomach aches (and, in the long term, to the development of more serious conditions, such as peptic ulcers).

- *Problems sleeping.* This is also indicative of psychological stress; it may be manifested in a reluctance to go to bed in the evenings (coupled with a reluctance to get up in the mornings), general insomnia (indicative of anxiety), reports/evidence of the young person suffering from nightmares or (more rarely) bed-wetting or sleepwalking.

Unfortunately, this is not a fail-proof checklist. The presence of some of these things, or even all of them, doesn't necessarily mean that the young person is being bullied. After all, there can be (say) reluctance to go to school for a number of reasons, and the numerous trials of adolescence can mean that teenagers develop signs of stress, such as problems sleeping, changes in mood, headaches and stomach aches. However, if these signs and symptoms persist, as a responsible parent, one would undoubtedly suspect something serious was wrong, and thus investigate the matter further.

Practically speaking, 'investigation' of most, if not all, these factors will mean talking to the young person. This is not always easy, for reasons which have been partially outlined above. There may be tremendous reluctance on the part of a bullied person to 'tell' anyone about the behaviour he or she is suffering. However, we have outlined some hints and strategies below ('What to do if your child/teenager is being bullied') by which the problem of a young person being bullied can be approached by a concerned parent. Even if not resolving the issue, such a 'talk' can at least prove helpful in establishing what has gone on and working towards countering the bullying behaviour that the young person is experiencing.

WHAT TO DO IF YOUR CHILD/TEENAGER IS BEING BULLIED

Finding out what's wrong

Finding out that our child or teenager has been bullied is very difficult. As parents we are caught between our desire to help and protect our offspring, and the dread and discomfort of hearing that our children/teenagers are suffering. The news that a young person is being bullied leaves his or her parent with a confusing mix of emotions: upset, sadness, anger; feeling that one has failed to protect one's child; and impotence to resolve the issue (if the victimization is happening at school). Yet it is vital for us, as grown-ups, to contain these feelings; we can be consoled by the fact that by the structured support of our child/teenager, and collaboration with his or her school, that we can do something positive about the situation. The first step towards this, however, is to find out what has been going on.

The best advice we can give parents is first, to make yourself available, and to ask your child/teenager if anything has been troubling him or her. Just letting the young person know that you are there for him or her may be helpful in itself; although he or she may not be ready to tell you, the knowledge that he or she can, and that you as a parent care and are motivated to help, can come as a relief. Repeated questioning (no matter how gently put) can impart the flavour of inter-rogation rather than concern: therefore, where possible and appropriate, let the young person tell you in his or her own time. It may, of course, be necessary to be more persistent if the young person is in serious distress or danger. Parents should not be afraid to acknowledge that they, too, may have been bullied.

Secondly, a parent must be prepared to both listen and talk, but to do rather more of the former than the latter. We have been given two ears, but only one mouth, after all! Listening closely to young people communicates our acceptance, warmth and care towards them; it is also vital in building self-esteem. If the young person feels that he or she has been bullied, acknowledge this. Parents will, quite naturally and as a result of the love they have for their children, want to 'do something'. Some ideas around this – that is, what one might say, or do in order to help a bul-lied young person – are included in the paragraphs immediately below.

The bully has the problem, not the victim

One of the most important things that a parent can do for a bullied young person is to assure him or her that it is not he or she who has the problem, but the person who is bullying them. This fact seems obvious to us, as adults; however, one should remember two key facts. First, those who bully can be extremely manipulative; secondly, a pattern that is common to all patterns of abuse is that the abuser encourages the person who he or she abuses to internalize the prob-lem. In other words, although it may seem almost shocking to state it so bluntly, the person being bullied is made to believe, at least at some level, that he or she deserves or invites the abuse he or she suffers from. Primary school aged chil-dren may lament, 'Oh, if only I were taller/shorter/fatter/thinner/didn't wear glasses/had a different hair colour/didn't have freckles/spoke differently/were better at (insert name of sport/activity) *then* I wouldn't get picked on!' In other words, because those who bully typically single out a person for being somehow 'different' – please note, this so-called difference may be real or imaginary, as the many heterosexuals who have been bullied for being 'gay' will testify – the victim comes to believe (or is made to, through the abuse of the bullying process) that it is this 'difference' that causes or invites the bullying. Hence, people who have been persistently made fun of due to their hair colour may attempt to change this; the high achiever, labelled a 'swot', deliberately sabotages his or her own results; the short-sighted student, ridiculed for his or her style of glasses, removes them and thus cannot see the board in lessons. Pitifully, we have even heard tell of a very young black girl who, ridiculed by her white classmates as being 'dirty', attempted to scrub off the colour of her skin with lavatory cleaner, causing more than superficial tissue damage in the process.

Hence, one can be bullied 'for' anything. Bullying is, therefore, always the bully's fault, and the problem lies with him or her; in other words, abuse is always the fault of the abuser. However, the aforementioned 'internalization' can be exacerbated by the ongoing eradication of self-esteem that is fostered by being victimized. We deal with the critical issue of self-esteem below.

Don't fight back physically!

In days gone by, well-meaning adults would often dispense the advice that the best thing to do when one was hit was to hit back, on the grounds that 'bullies are cowards, and will run away if you fight them'. However, there are two very good reasons as to why this traditional advice is wrong, and will almost certainly worsen the situation should the young person act upon it. First, as the Australian expert Ken Rigby[3] points out, many bullies like a good fight, are not physical cowards and do not always back down. Hence, whilst a victim's stand against his or her aggressor might in a way be admirable in terms of courage, the end result may be a particularly severe physical beating – a continuation and worsening of the bullying situation.

Secondly, as we mentioned above, many people who bully are deft manipulators of the school discipline system. If it happens that the person who is bullied is physically stronger than the bully, or for some reason comes off best in the 'showdown' with the person who has bullied him or her, the bully may then perhaps engage his or her friend in a false report, claiming that he or she has been the persecuted party – and so the school ends up disciplining the wrong person.

Teaching coping skills

It is worthwhile explaining to the bullied young person that bullies *want* an upset reaction. Humour, silence or an assertive response – that is, standing up for oneself in a non-aggressive way – may well prevent a further attack.

Action suggestion 4.1: coping with verbal abuse/bullying

People   You (parent), your son(s)/daughter(s)

Materials   None

Method   Essentially, the parent here acts as a 'coach' to his or her child /teenager, trying to develop methods by which a young person can avoid, deflect or cope with verbal harassment and bullying. Some people might anticipate using role-play here; however, we would advocate having the parent(s) and young person as collaborators on a joint 'action plan'. The idea is to generate methods by which the young person can avoid, deflect or cope with verbal attacks made upon him or her; hence, as the young person must imagine (or remember) such attacks being made upon him or her, he or she might feel rather vulnerable. The parent(s) should proceed with as much sensitivity as possible, supporting the young person if he or she becomes upset. It is always important to consider, and to keep in mind constantly, whether the long-term benefit of generating coping strategies outweighs, at any given time, the costs of asking the young person to think of something that is by and large unpleasant and potentially distressing.

The main options are:

1 *The silent treatment*. This could include:

    (a) Avoiding the person who is bullying or harassing you altogether.

    (b) Walking away (not running away) from the bully if you see them coming.

    (c) Completely ignoring it when someone is calling you names – pretending that you haven't heard them at all. It's difficult not to give any response, but possible; this can even be turned into a game when practising at home.

2 *Humour*. This can work in the case of name-calling/verbal bullying only. This could include:

    (a) Thinking of a witty response (get some ready at home).

    (b) Acting as if it doesn't bother you, by literally laughing it off (difficult, but possible). Remember, people who bully are generally looking for an upset reaction; if you don't give them one, they are likely to stop, or choose someone else who does get upset to victimize.

CONTINUED

3 *Assertiveness*. This could include:

(a) Standing up straight, looking confident, speaking clearly and firmly, maintaining eye contact (always), and telling the person bullying you to stop.

(b) Telling the person bullying you that you don't care what they think of you, and that calling you names isn't going to get you upset.

(c) Taking ownership of what the person doing the bullying thinks will upset you, for example, 'So what if I'm short? I don't mind it at all', 'So what if I wear glasses? I think they look great.' We are also, at this point, reminded of the case of an Irish boy (we'll call him John) whose parents moved to England, where he was persistently verbally bullied on the grounds of his nationality. John tried to laugh it off, or ignore it, but these things did not work. Eventually, one day he said, 'So what if I'm Irish? I live here now, but I'm proud of where I come from!' The people bullying him could not think of a nasty response to this very reasonable statement of fact.

Together, a parent and young person can choose any of these, or a combination, as seems appropriate to the situation that the young bullied person typically finds himself or herself in. The young person can describe a situation that he or she has experienced, or is particularly afraid of experiencing, and together with his or her parent, see which of the above tactics would work.

Please note that there is no way to 'laugh off', or to use humour/assertion with regards to serious physical assaults. These are illegal, and should always be reported to the appropriate school (and, if necessary, external) authorities.

The importance of self-esteem (part 1)

A good deal of evidence from psychological and educational research exists to show that a person's involvement in bullying behaviour (as either a perpetrator or a victim) is fairly strongly linked to his or her level of self-esteem. In general, we can say that school students who are bullied, or who bully others, have lower self-esteem than people who are not involved in bullying behaviour, and that the more often one has been bullied, or has bullied others, the lower is one's levels of self-esteem.[4]

Self-esteem is built in people from early childhood, and is associated with what can be called 'positive parenting'. Positive (or self-esteem building) parenting includes showing love and respect for the young person through verbal and non-verbal demonstrations of appropriate affection and encouragement, and ensuring that a sense of security for the young person is provided in the home, and that he or she is not subjected to either neglect nor any form of abuse. It also involves setting firm boundaries and rules for the young person. These limits should be negotiable within the limits of what is in the young person's own best interests, rather than what the young person decides he or she feels like doing at any one time. Young people should be involved in day-to-day decisions, but not over-loaded with responsibility inappropriate to either his or her age or family role, and realistic expectations should be set. A young person should be praised when he or she does something well; however, remember that praise should be gen-uine, and appropriate to the amount of effort the young person has made, and never 'over the top' or effusive.

Action suggestion 4.2: building self-esteem at home

People   You (parent)

Materials: None

Method   Very simply, read over the material in the paragraphs immedi-ately above, and take a few minutes to think about your own experiences of being parented (that is, when you were a child yourself), and of parenting others (that is, how you relate to your own children/teenagers). To what extent could these rela-tionships be described as 'positive' or 'self-esteem enhancing' parenting? Then think of a few practical ways in which the self-esteem enhancing strategies outlined in the five points immediately above could be incorporated into how you relate to your children/teenagers on a day-to-day basis. Is your par-enting style already self-esteem enhancing? If not, do you need to make any changes?

Reporting the problem

Naturally, whilst parental support is extremely helpful to a bullied young person, there is a limit to what a parent can do if their child is being victimized at school. So in most, if not all, cases it makes sense for contact between the home and the school about resolving the bullying situation to be established. However, there are a number of reasons as to why this might be difficult, and a number of things parents will need to know before reporting the bullying that their children/teenagers have suffered to the school authorities. For this reason, we have devoted an entire section of this chapter to 'Working with your child's/teenager's school against bullying' (see below).

WHAT TO DO IF YOUR CHILD/TEENAGER IS BULLYING OTHERS

Awareness of what bullying is

A critical aspect to remember here is that whilst a young person who is being bullied often recognizes (at least) that something unpleasant is happening to him or her, even if he or she doesn't recognize that he or she has been bullied, a young person who is involved in bullying others may not even realize that what he or she is doing is experienced as unpleasant by the person who is being victimized, let alone constitutes bullying. Therefore, if a young person has been accused of bullying someone else and is honestly unable to understand why he or she has been so accused, a good first step for parents might be to discuss the material in 'The different types of bullying' in the section, 'What parents need to know' above, and attempt to relate the different categories of bullying and examples to his or her own behaviour (if necessary, as perceived by the person being bullied).

Be a good role model

People learn an astonishing amount of behaviour during their early childhood years through the imitation of the behaviour of those whom they see around them. It is important to remember that, as parents, we teach our children both intentionally (through what we tell them, the advice we give, the lessons we teach, the spoken values we try to instil and so on) and unintentionally – by providing them with a model to copy (psychologists call this process of learning from a model 'social learning'). Hence, a child's views on and strategies for coping with aggression will, to an extent, be determined by what he or she has observed at home, as well being partially shaped by his or her experiences in the peer group and at school. It is therefore critical to consider what a child might be learning from you as a parent in terms of analysing your own ways of coping with anger and conflict in the home.

Action suggestion 4.3: how do I model coping with aggression?

People	You (parent)
Materials	None
Method	First, read over and think about the material outlined in the paragraph immediately above. Take a few minutes to think about the following questions, and answer them as honestly as you can.

1 How do I react when I am angry, annoyed or upset?

2 How do my reactions to anger, annoyance or upset affect other people? In particular, how do they affect my children/teenagers?

CONTINUED

3 How do the young people in my household react when they are angry, annoyed or upset? Where did they learn this style of reaction?

4 What messages around aggression, harassment and violence have my children/teenagers been exposed to in terms of their parenting relationship with me?

5 What messages around aggression, harassment and violence have my children/teenagers been exposed to from other sources (that is, other relations, friends, neighbours and especially the media)?

6 What values and attitudes around aggression, harassment and violence do my children/teenagers hold, and how are these attitudes expressed in their behaviour?

The goal of this exercise is to consider how you as a parent have modelled attitudes towards anger, annoyance, upset, aggression, violence and harassment, and the expression of these behaviourally, to your children/teenagers. Do you think you need to make any changes?

Finding out what's wrong

The basic guidelines about being there for the young person, listening and talking with them has already been outlined (see the corresponding 'Finding out what's wrong', in the 'What to do if your child/teenager is being bullied' section above). There are just a few general points to note when we consider what might happen when a child/teenager is accused of bullying. First, for whatever reason, it is possible that the young person might not have been involved at all.

Equally, the young person might have been involved, but may not realize that his or her actions were experienced by the victim as bullying/aggression/harassment. Hence, the thing to be done here is to make the person aware of both what bullying is, and how this has been matched with his or her own behaviour, and to point out the undesirability of this behaviour.

It is also possible that the young person might have been involved, and may be unrepentant about having been so. Here, attitudes will need to be challenged with the goal of behavioural change. Guidelines for talking to young people who have been involved as perpetrators of bullying behaviour are included in the paragraphs immediately below. As parents, we don't like to believe that bad things are true of our child/teenager, or his or her behaviour. If, for example, a group of teenage boys are involved in an anti-social act in the community (let us say, vandalism of public property), it is likely that most parents will blame the other teenagers for leading their son astray. And despite the positive parenting influence that we try to have on them, sometimes our offspring do get involved in behaviour that we would sooner they did not.

Just as there is no 'typical' picture of a victim of bullying behaviour (one can be singled out for any 'reason', real or imagined), there is no 'typical' picture of a young person who engages in bullying behaviour. As far as we know, bullying behaviour occurs amongst children of every social class, age, race and religion; it occurs in rural and urban areas, areas of both high and low unemployment, and in schools and classes of all sizes.

However, it is possible to say that a genuinely happy child doesn't go around picking on others. Young people who are involved in bullying may be upset about something, either at school or in the home. Separation, divorce, a change in the family's social or economic situation or make-up; conflict with friends and acquaintances; disappointment in academic or social life; an experience of having been bullied oneself, and this not having been dealt with effectively – all these things can, and sometimes do, precipitate a loss of self-esteem in young people, which may be manifested in involvement as a perpetrator of harassment, bullying or aggressive behaviour.

When we hear that our child/teenager has been involved in bullying behaviour, we may feel disappointed in him or her; we may feel that we have failed ourselves as parents; we may feel angry at our child's/teenager's friends, or the friends' parents, for the bad influence we might suppose our child's/teenager's peers have had on him or her. This set of emotions can often lead us, in such situations, to express anger; and yet, with everything we have already said about modelling a controlled response to conflict and aggression (see above), this is precisely the wrong thing to do. As with the parent who has heard that his or her child has been victimized, the best thing to do is to contain such feelings until we have found a way to intervene that helps and supports our child/teenager, whilst (if he or she has indeed been involved in bullying others) challenging and changing the young person's attitudes, and the expression of such aggressive and victimizing behaviour.

The importance of self-esteem (part 2)

Some people are surprised to find out that, according to recent research evidence, perpetrators of bullying share their victims' lowered levels of self-esteem; indeed, the more often one bullies others, the lower is one's level of self-esteem. Bullying others can, then, be seen as a misguided attempt to gain self-esteem (perhaps in the form of peer recognition) – hence, it is perhaps predictable that bullied school students, their parents and their teachers will often say (and perhaps correctly so) that a bully's behaviour is due to their 'showing off', 'jealousy' or 'looking for attention'.

Some young people are involved in bullying behaviour as both perpetrators and victims; sometimes such a person is involved in victimising another, and sometimes he or she is on the receiving end of such treatment. Such people are typically referred to by anti-bullying researchers as bully-victims, and this pattern of behaviour is surprisingly common. In itself, this challenges traditional notions of the 'hawks and doves' idea that has long been held. Relationships in student populations of people where bullying takes place are not necessarily dyadic, split between persistent and regular aggressors and passive victims. Instead, it seems that there are some people (the bully-victims) who preserve their own safety status by joining in the persecution of others. It is therefore unsurprising to note that in the aforementioned research, bully-victims had the lowest levels of self-esteem – lower than victims who did not bully, bullies who were never victimized and students who were not involved in bullying behaviour at all.[5]

We have included some guidelines and ideas by which parents can help to build self-esteem in young people in the section above (see 'The importance of self-esteem (Part 1', especially 'Action suggestion 4.2). These ideas should also be of use to parents whose primary concern is their child's/teenager's involvement in bullying others. As indicated previously, children of medium or high self-esteem tend not to be involved in bullying behaviour as either perpetrators or victims; it is therefore to be hoped that by building self-esteem, young people can be 'insulated' against involvement in bullying behaviour.

Teaching empathy

Empathy is the capacity to literally and accurately understand how another person feels; it is therefore distinct from sympathy, which more often involves merely feeling sorry for someone's misfortunes. People differ in terms of how well their capacity for empathy is developed. For example, there are some people whom we know to be good listeners – when we talk to them, say about a problem or a matter that concerns us, we feel as though such a person has tried (and succeeded) to understand and support us, without necessarily having dispensed 'advice' to us. Such a person could be described as having shown empathy, or more accurately empathic concern, towards us. It is for this reason that many counsellors value the capacity to show empathic concern towards their clients above all of their other therapeutic skills.

The critical point here is that if one can empathize with another – or 'put oneself in another's shoes' – then one is unlikely to victimize that other person. Some psychologists have come to feel that 'empathy is an antidote to aggression'. Certainly, it is important to encourage a person who is bullying others to consider, 'How would it feel if someone else were bullying you?' However, before we get to this point, there are some important factors that we should consider. As stated above, some people are more empathetic than others. As a parent, when we hear any child crying, our (what seems to be our natural instinctive) response is to find out what is wrong with the child, then to seek to find some way or someone to comfort the child. But how 'instinctive' is this response? Did we not, in fact, learn this response somewhere else? Perhaps when we first took charge of our own offspring, or those of a close friend or relative?

Let us consider, then, for the sake of comparison, the responses (both empathic and non-empathic) of children. Children show empathic concern for an initially astonishingly small circle of relations, acquaintances and even objects, but this circle widens over the years. For example, in late infancy, a child might literally climb over a sibling (perhaps even causing some pain to that sibling) in order to thrust a teddy bear towards a parent, complaining somewhat tearfully that Teddy is 'sad' because he didn't get a 'goodnight kiss'. In the early school years, a crying child, unless he or she is one's friend or sibling, may provoke not concern, but a feeling that he or she is 'different', 'weird' or even 'soft'. It seems then that a child will feel sad for their friend's or sibling's tears, but not necessarily for those of someone he or she doesn't know, or knows only vaguely. This, being practically universal in Western cultures, is not a fault in children, but one of the limits that children have when compared with adults – just as they are likely to find reading, writing and mathematical tasks more difficult than do their parents, so they are less likely to feel empathic concern for someone whom they do not know. In any event, empathic concern is not a capacity that one can rely on young people to have – and so, if it is to be used at all as a means by which a tendency to bully others can be countered, empathy must be taught. So how does one, as a parent, 'teach' empathy to young people?

Action suggestion 4.4: teaching skills of empathy

People	You (parent), your son(s) / daughter(s)
Materials	None
Method	Young people will be prepared to discuss their hobbies or interests (perhaps given some prompting!): some might be interested in sport; others, music; still others, computer games. Most young people have a favourite film or set of films, or television programme(s), or are capable of discussing material they have seen in films or on the television. The key to this activity is nothing more than in the course of such discussions, asking some well-placed questions that focus the young person on the sportsman's/musician's/actor's feelings and inner motivations – that is, encouraging the young person to think about how the person under discussion feels, and why he does what he does.

For example, it could be that a young person enjoys soccer – in this case he or she will almost certainly have a favourite team and a favourite player – and has been watching an important match. Unless the match has resulted in a draw, one team will have won, and the other team will have lost. Some questions that could be discussed are as follows:

1   How do you think that the winning captain feels? (Not just 'good' or 'great', but at a deeper level as well – help the young person with words if he or she doesn't know/use them already).

2   If you were the winning captain, and were to be interviewed by the television commentators, what would you say to the fans?

3   How does it feel when you come out 'on top'? Has this happened recently? If so, when, what happened, and how did it feel?

4   What do you understand by being 'modest in success', and is it important? Why is this? How do other people feel when people are boastful?

5   How do you think that the losing captain feels? (Not just 'bad' or 'terrible', but again, at a deeper level as well – and again, help the young person with words if he or she doesn't know/use them already.)

6   If you were the losing captain, what words of encouragement could you find for your teammates in the dressing room?

7   How does it feel when you come out 'at the bottom'? Has this happened recently? If so, when, what happened, and how did it feel?

8   What do you understand by being 'gracious in defeat', and is this important? Why is this? How do other people feel when people are 'sore losers'?

This sort of exercise can obviously be adjusted for discussing feelings around success and setbacks in other areas of social life in which your young people might have an interest. The important things are:

1   To focus the young person on discussing feelings, rather than events.

2   The development of a vocabulary around discussing emotions.

3   Thinking through both success and setbacks – giving the child the opportunity to mentally experience and think through both.

Teaching respect for differences

Bullying is, almost universally, directed against a victim whom, by consent of those perpetrating the bullying, is different in some (real or imagined) way. It is perhaps not surprising that bullying should take place in secondary schools, given the enormous importance that conforming to one's peer group has to teenagers. Despite the fact that this conformity is disputed and disavowed by adolescents, adults looking back on this period will acknowledge it, and sometimes express slight shock at the way in which they dressed and the things that they held to be true. It is also true that whatever we may believe about the value of the individual in free democratic society that even the most non-conventional of us feels at least some need to 'fit in' (even if this 'fitting in' is to the values of a counter-cultural subgroup): we experience a deep need to belong. Society transmits this very effectively to young children and, perhaps with their concomitant emotional needs for security, even the youngest children like to be amongst their group of friends. Sadly, the shadow side of this 'in-grouping' is, of course, 'out-grouping' – the exclusion of those who don't fit into our group, and sometimes the active persecution of those who are somehow 'different' to us. This tendency is so strong that many people who are involved in bullying others believe that what they are doing is correct; that they are legitimately 'teaching them a lesson' or 'straightening them out'. Should we be tempted to be critical of young people for holding this set of attitudes, we should remember that armed conflict is often started along precisely the same lines of 'reasoning'.

The fact that we can achieve an understanding of this process does not mean that such behaviour is to be condoned. In order to prevent and counter bullying behaviour on the basis of perceived differences, there needs to be a greater tolerance and respect of individual differences. Of course, there are limits to acceptance of individual differences – such as when they infringe upon the human rights of others.

Action suggestion 4.5: teaching respect for differences

People You (parent), your son(s)/daughter(s)

Materials None

Method As in Action suggestion 4.4, this consists of nothing more sophisticated than discussing a young person's hobbies and interests, or material seen in films or on the television, with the inclusion of a few well-placed questions.

The important thing here is to find a person or people to discuss, at a surface level, that the young person is unlikely to feel he or she has much in common with. It is always easier for young people, in the initial phases of considering another person outside the friendship/peer group, to consider what is different about someone.

A typical example might be the discussion of a news item involving people from a country and culture different from the young person's own. Focus not on the politicians and leaders, but on a single 'ordinary person' depicted in the broadcast. Some useful things to discuss might be as follows:

1 What do you have in common with this person?

2 Who does this person live with, and in what sort of house?

CONTINUED

3 (For adults) What do you think this person does for a living (Or, for children and teenagers) Where does this person go to school, and what is his or her school like?

4 What do you think constitutes this person's daily routine? What is your daily routine? How do the two compare?

5 What do you think this person would like to do tomorrow? What are his or her hopes, dreams and ambitions for next year? The next five years? For his or her children?

6 Assuming there were no language barriers, what would you like to ask him or her? And what do you think he or she would like to ask you?

7 Do you think that you could get to like this person?

Hence, the overall aims are:

1 To find a gradually more sophisticated answer to the first question, 'What do you have in common with this person?'

2 To counter, or at least to challenge, the stereotypical pattern of focusing on differences, rather than similarities, when we first consider or think about someone we have not met before;

3 To promote the idea that as human beings, despite superficial differences, we have more in common than we generally think (at least at first).

Letting off steam in a positive way

The idea of catharsis, or the relieving effect of release of energy that is somehow 'trapped' in the body (or indeed, the mind), is an old one (going back millennia to the philosophers of Ancient Greece), and it is a concept that psychologists have used in the treatment of their clients, in a variety of senses and contexts, for about the last 100 years. Of course, one does not have to have designated oneself in need of psychological help to make the concept work. It is a fact of life that some people are, perhaps due to their biological make-up, more energetic, or aggressive than others, just as some are taller or slimmer than others. Hence, some children find themselves getting into trouble owing to their natural energy spilling over into roughness, or their inability/inopportunity to find ways to cope with their aggressiveness. It is, therefore, important for such young people to find ways of 'letting off steam' in a safe and pro-social way. On asking, 'Well, why did you do it?' ('it' being some anti-social or illegal act), many of us have received a response along the lines of, 'I was bored'. By using such young people's reasoning, it occurs to us (as indeed the young people in question are contending) that if they had not been bored, then the anti-social or illegal behaviour would not have taken place. Hence, some form of a creative or positive recreational activity seems to be a good idea.

Competitive team sports (for example, soccer, rugby, hockey, netball, basketball and so on) are a good way for a young person to learn about team-building, rules, and pro-social behaviour such as co-operation and support, as well as a controlled way of releasing energy and aggression. Solo sports and activities (for example, walking, swimming, skiing, cycling and running), whilst lacking the pro-social element, at least provide the opportunity for releasing anger and aggression. The philosophy of martial arts teaches people about the need for the control of aggression, as most of these techniques must only be used as a last resort in situations of self-defence. Remember also that people can also express themselves emotionally through the arts – drawing, painting, acting, rapping/singing, musicianship, drama and film-making.

Whilst being popular amongst young people, hobbies such as computer games, the use of the Internet, watching television and the cinema can have, quite obviously, no real role in creating conditions for the safe expression of aggression and excess energy, being extremely passive by nature. Indeed, it is advisable, given the aggressive content of certain games/films/websites/television programmes, that parents might wish to limit, or certainly monitor their children's/teenagers' involvement in such pursuits.

WORKING WITH YOUR CHILD'S/TEENAGER'S SCHOOL AGAINST BULLYING

Reporting to the school: what you and your child/teenager will want and need to know

When parents say to young people that the matter of their having been bullied should be reported to the school, a situation of high emotion can result. The young person may beg or plead with the parent not to tell, feeling (and almost certainly expressing) that the situation will be made worse, primarily through the person who has bullied him or her finding out about the report and seeking retribution. The parent may be told that this is 'grassing' (also called 'clyping', 'squealing', 'ratting', 'snitching' or 'telling tales', depending on where you live), and that is the worst thing that a person can do, and be accused of having betrayed the young person's confidence. In short, the young person may display a combination of highly charged emotions – rage, alarm, fear, distrust and a feeling of abandonment.

However, sometimes the young person must be overruled. This can be the case if the child is likely, through further exposure to the ongoing situation of bullying/harassment, to experience serious risks to his or her physical or psychological health. Sometimes, after all, we have to overrule our child/teenager on other matters; and parenting is not about winning a popularity contest, but doing what is in the young person's best interests. Of course, in overruling the young person, and risking his or her (at least short-term) wrath, we have to be sure that what we are doing really is in his or her best interests, and the only reason that we can see why this is the case, and the young person can't, is due to our greater experience and maturity – and not because we are simply responding blindly to our need as parents to 'do something'. Hence, we must be sure that the school will handle the matter in a sensitive and responsible way.

For some years, experts in the countering of bullying, aggressive behaviour and harassment have been advocating that schools have a written code of behaviour and discipline that specifies how bullying should be reported and dealt with in the school. Thankfully, owing to governmental and focus group initiatives, most schools do have such a code. This code should specify (1) how bullying behaviour is defined and understood by the school staff and management authorities; (2) how a complaint of bullying behaviour is to be recorded and investigated; (3) what action will be taken in terms of sanctions against the perpetrators of the bullying behaviour; (4) what support structures exist for both the victim and the perpetrator of the bullying behaviour; and (5) what policies and strategies exist for the ongoing practise of countering and preventing bullying behaviour.

As a parent you should be assured (as your child/teenager will want reassurance) that the incident and report will be treated in a sensitive manner; that confidentiality will be kept as much as possible; and, that your child/teenager will be safeguarded, as far as it is possible, against further incidents of bullying behaviour (in particular, that the perpetrator of the bullying will be prevented from making retributive acts against the child/teenager, or his or her parent/s, who have made the report).

You as a parent should be kept informed about the progress of this case. Parents should be aware that investigating an allegation of bullying behaviour in such a sensitive and thorough manner may well be time-consuming. As parents, when we hear that our child/teenager has been bullied, the young person has in most cases been bullied for several months or years already, having kept this secret from everyone. Hence, although we might want instantaneous results on reporting such an incident – 'Isn't x months of suffering enough already?', parents must be prepared to be patient in order for the school to do as effective an investigation and intervention as possible. However, we would reiterate that as a parent you do have a right to be updated and informed of the progress that a school is making in dealing with a case of bullying, and to be confident that the case is being dealt with in the shortest possible time frame.

Parent–school collaboration against bullying behaviour

Many schools have a parents' council, or parents'–teachers' association. Activity in such an organization (if one doesn't exist already, contact the school and other parents in your local community with a view to setting one up) is a great forum by which a concerned parent can bring to the attention of his or her fellow parents the issues of bullying, aggressive behaviour and harassment, and begin to start action on this issue. A good school thrives on the relationship it has with its local community. It is, in a way, a tragedy which all too often occurs, when teachers and parents start blaming each other for the bullying and aggressive behaviour of young people, and end up on 'opposite sides of the fence'. For example: 'The school should do something if it's on their grounds and in school hours – what can we do, after all?' says one parent to another. 'We're dealing with stuff that's come into the school from the outside – what sort of an example are these kids being set at home, anyway?' says one disaffected teacher to another.

In successful broad-scale intervention approaches against bullying, the 'community' or 'whole-school' approach, has consistently been advocated. Parents, through a council or association, can indeed have an impact on the schools' action upon issues of bullying, aggressive behaviour and harassment. Parents should be consulted on matters of school planning, and the drafting of new or revised school policy/codes; when so consulted, they should take this role seriously, bringing attention to matters that concern them (in this case, bullying behaviour). Parents' organizations can themselves fund and source guest speakers for information evenings, and co-fund or partake in ongoing preventative measures against bullying behaviour – 'Anti-bullying weeks', and so on. Parents can, and indeed should, organizing themselves if necessary, ensure that their local communities are 'bully-free'. If parents expect that bullying should be prevented during school hours and inside school grounds, then they can play their part in ensuring that victimization is not simply pushed out of the school gates and into the local area.

Hopefully, this chapter, and particularly this latter section, has been helpful in supplying ideas and means by which parents and school personnel can collaborate – forming a strong alliance of responsible and caring adults, with the common concern of preventing and countering bullying, aggressive behaviour and harassment amongst young people in schools.

SUMMARY

- In the first section of this chapter, 'What parents need to know', the different types of bullying, why parents are so important, and a 'checklist' of signs and symptoms of being bullied were presented.

- In the second section, 'What to do if your child/teenager is being bullied', parents were given advice on finding out what's wrong (where they suspect that their child/teenager has been bullied); reassuring the bullied person that it is the bully who has the problem, not the victim; the importance of not fighting back physically; teaching young people to develop coping skills; and, building self-esteem in young people at home.

- In the third major section, 'What to do if your child/teenager is bullying others', advice was given to parents on creating an awareness of what bullying is; the importance of being a good role model; how to find out what's wrong; the importance of self-esteem; teaching empathy and respect for differences; and, means by which young people can let off steam in a positive way.

- In the final section, 'Working with your child's/teenager's school against bullying', a series of points designed to cover what you and your child/teenager will want and need to know was covered, along with practical ways in which parents and schools can collaborate against bullying behaviour.

FURTHER RESOURCES FOR PARENTS

Elliot, M. (1997) *101 Ways to Deal with Bullying: A Guide for Parents*. London: Hodder & Stoughton.

Lawson, S. (1995) *Helping Children Cope with Bullying*. London: Sheldon Press.

O' Donnell, V. (1995) *Bullying: A Resource Guide for Parents and Teachers*. Dublin: Attic Press

Chapter 5

What all young people need to know

WHAT'S IN THIS CHAPTER

This chapter has been written especially for young people who are concerned about bullying. However, we think that every young person should know about bullying in schools. When we wrote this chapter, we tried to write it for older children and teenagers. These are people who are old enough to be able to read and understand the chapter themselves. If you are younger than this, please ask your mother or father, or whoever looks after you at home, to help you. You can also tell them that Chapter 4 of this book has been written especially for them. Here is a list of things that we want to talk about in this chapter:

- What every young person needs to know about bullying

- What to do if you are being bullied

- How you can help prevent bullying in your school.

WHAT EVERY YOUNG PERSON NEEDS TO KNOW ABOUT BULLYING

What is bullying?

How do we know when something that is happening should be called bullying?

- Bullying is deliberate. The bully or bullies are trying to upset or hurt the person that they are bullying in some way, on purpose.

- Bullying involves singling out a person for bad treatment.

- Bullying is something that is repeated. The person being bullied is picked on again and again, sometimes for a very long time.

- The person being bullied either can not or will not defend himself or herself. This is one of the reasons why bullying is so unfair.

- It is not bullying every time people quarrel. If two people of about the same age, size and strength, have the occasional fight or quarrel, it is not bullying.

We can put all of these ideas into two sentences that will tell us what bullying is, and what bullying is not:

We say that a student is being bullied when he or she is singled out *in an* unpleasant way *by another student or group of students. The bullied student is* picked on again and again, *and it is* difficult *for the person being bullied to defend himself or herself. It is* not *bullying when young people of about the same age and power have the occasional fight or quarrel.*

Some people think that we can only call it bullying when someone is hurt physically, but this is not true. In most types of bullying, the person being bullied is not hit or kicked or even touched at all. However, all types of bullying hurt people's feelings, which is just as bad as being hurt physically. We are now going to describe the different types of bullying.

The different types of bullying

Here is a list of some different types of bullying:

- *Verbal bullying.* This is when someone calls another person nasty names, or teases them or jokes about them in a cruel way. This can hurt someone's feelings a lot. This sort of teasing and name-calling is particularly nasty if it is about someone's family, race or religion, or about the way they look.

- *Physical bullying.* This can involve slapping, pushing, shoving, kicking, poking, elbowing, kneeing, tripping up, punching or hitting the person being bullied with weapons or other objects. It is also physical bullying when a bully deliberately damages the bullied person's clothes or other personal property.

- *Threatening.* Sometimes a bully will threaten the person they are being bullied – 'We will get you after school', and things like that.

- *Gesture bullying.* Gestures are messages that we send without speaking. Some gestures can be threatening, and are used by bullies. These include shaking fists, and looks or glances that contain nasty messages.

- *Extortion.* This means taking money or personal property from the person being bullied. Sometimes, bullies will force a person to steal things for them, or to break or vandalize property. The bully will threaten to 'tell' on the person who was forced to steal or break things.

- *Ignoring someone, or always leaving them out of things.* If the same person is always left out of games, activities or conversations, then this is also bullying.

- *Trying to make others dislike someone.* In this type of bullying, the bully or bullies try to make the person being bullied unpopular. This can involve spreading lies about someone, or spreading rumours or gossip. Bullies can also threaten other students, and make them leave the person being bullied out of things – 'If you talk to … , we'll get you next'. This means that other people are afraid to be seen talking to the person being bullied, and the bullied person ends up feeling even more lonely.

- *Writing or drawing nasty things about someone.* This can involve sending round nasty notes about or drawings of the person being bullied. It can also include the writing of insulting graffiti on blackboards, or in public places.

- *E-bullying.* This is sending threatening or nasty e-mail or text messages, or creating a website for hate messages about someone.

As you can see, there are many different types of bullying. Can you think of any that we did not include?

WHAT TO DO IF YOU ARE BEING BULLIED

Talking to adults about being bullied – why it's so important and how to do it

If you are being bullied, and you want it to stop, you *must* tell an adult you trust – a family member, whoever looks after you at home, or someone in the school (a teacher or other staff member that you get on well with). Telling someone you have been bullied is absolutely necessary, and also one of the hardest things to do in the world. This is why we've put our thoughts down about this below. So, please remember:

- Young people who have been bullied need the help of their families and schools. No one can deal with being bullied on his or her own.

- Hoping that the bullying will somehow 'go away' will not work. The situation will almost certainly get worse if you stay silent, because the bully realizes that he or she can get away with it.

- No one can help you unless you tell someone that you have been bullied – your family and teachers are not mind-readers.

- Bullies usually don't just pick on one person. So by coming forward and letting someone know that you have been bullied, you are helping others as well as yourself.

- And, most importantly – there is nothing wrong in telling an adult that you or someone else has been bullied. In telling someone, you are behaving in a very responsible way.

Many people are afraid of telling someone that they have been bullied because they think that the bullying will get worse if they do. They think that the bully will find out who 'told' and will want revenge. They think that they will be called nasty names if they 'tell' on the bully. There is a big pressure against 'telling the teacher', particularly in secondary school. People who tell the teacher about things that go on between students may be called a 'tell-tale', or worse names, such as a 'grass', 'rat', 'snitch' or 'clype' (the names are all nasty, but different depending on where you live). Please remember one thing, though: telling the teacher that you or someone else has been bullied is *not* the same thing as being a 'tell-tale'.

In order to understand this, you have to think about why someone tells. A 'tell-tale' is someone who tells an adult something just to get someone else into trouble. The 'tell-tale' finds this funny in some way. This is not a nice thing to do.

Someone who tells an adult that he or she has been bullied is not a 'tell-tale'. He or she is telling because they want the bullying to stop, and not because he or she wants to get someone into trouble. It may be that the bully does get into trouble, but this is not because someone 'told'. It is because of the wrong thing – the bullying – that he or she did in the first place.

If you are unsure, or afraid of how the school might react to you reporting having been bullied, it's a good idea to tell someone at home first. The person at home can then find out from the school how they would deal with a case of bullying before making a report. There are some things that a parent or guardian, or whoever looks after you at home, should know about reporting an incident of bullying to a school. These are written in Chapter 4 of this book, which has been written especially for parents.

Remember, the bully has the problem, not you

One of the worst things about being bullied is that people who have been bullied are often made to feel that it is their own fault. This is not true. No one deserves to be bullied – there is no excuse for bullying others. Bullying is always wrong.

If we have been bullied, the bully (and others) can make us believe that it is our fault. This is because the name-calling or teasing that is involved in bullying is usually about something that is different about the person being bullied. People can be picked on because a bully will say that there is something wrong or different about:

- the bullied person's height (too short, or too tall) or weight (too thin, too heavy)

- the colour of the bullied person's skin, hair or eyes

- the religion, beliefs or nationality of the bullied person

- whether or not the bullied person wears glasses, uses a hearing aid, or uses a wheelchair

- the bullied person's abilities in lessons (too clever, or not clever enough) sports, games or activities

- the bullied person's clothes, personal hygiene, or other aspects of the bullied person's appearance

● the bullied person's family, friends or home life in general.

Can you think of any others?

So a bullied person might come to think that, 'Oh, if only I were taller/shorter/ fatter/thinner/didn't wear glasses/had a different hair colour/didn't have freckles/spoke differently/were better at, or did not do so well at (insert name of sport/activity) then I wouldn't get picked on!'

But this is not true. Where the bully can't find a difference, he or she will make one up. Many boys in school are bullied for being 'gay'. When adults use the word 'gay', they mean someone who is homosexual – someone who is romantically attracted to members of the same sex as himself or herself. Some young people use the word 'gay' to mean any boy who they don't like, or who doesn't fit in with their group, or group's ideas. Please remember that whether someone is homosexual or heterosexual is their own private business, and that people should never be bullied or treated badly because they are homosexual. The fact that bullies will say that someone is 'gay' because they can't find anything else that is 'different' about them shows that the bullying is always the bully's fault.

● Don't fight back physically!

Years ago, when your parents were children, adults would advise young people who had been bullied to hit the bullies back – to physically fight them off. They would say things like:

Bullies are cowards, and will run away if you fight them.

Unfortunately, we now know that this doesn't work. Yes, bullies are cowards, and that's why they pick on people who can't or won't fight back. But no, they will not run away from a fight, because bullies are usually aggressive people who like fighting.

The fact that bullies like, and are usually good at fighting, and the people they bully are the sort of people who do not like fighting, means that if you try and fight off a bully you will almost certainly lose. This means that if you are being physically bullied, and you try to fight the bully, 99 times out of 100 the beating you get will be even worse.

Even if something amazing happens – if by some miracle, the bullied person does win a physical fight against a bully – things can get a lot worse. This can happen in one of two ways:

● The bully can convince the school that you were the one who started the trouble. He or she can get his or her friends to tell lies to the school to back up his story. The school will almost certainly think that the fact that you won the fight is evidence that you started the problem.

● The bully can get together with his or her friends, and beat you up. Many people think that they can cope with being bullied by getting a gang together to beat up the bully or bullies. The only problem here is that violence only causes more violence. Think about this: I get beaten up by a bully, so I get my brother to beat up the bully. The bully then gets his brother and friends to beat up me and my brother. So I get all of my friends together, to beat up the bully, his brother and his friends. So then the bully gets … . Do you see how it goes on? This will lead to one or more of three things happening: someone ends up expelled from school; someone ends up in hospital; or someone ends up in trouble with the police. It's not worth it!

● How to cope if you are being verbally bullied

Please remember, that if you are being physically bullied, you must always tell someone. At school, it is the job of the school to deal with incidents of physical violence. At home or in the community, it is the job of parents to make sure that their children and teenagers are not physically hurting others. If incidents of physical violence at home or in the community are serious enough, then the police will have to be involved.

So, physical violence is something that you should never accept, or try to handle alone. But there are some things you can do about being verbally bullied.

You have to remember that bullies want an upset reaction from the people they bully. They want the bullied person to cry, get angry, become upset, or lose control. The bully and his or her friends will usually laugh at them when this happens. It seems to us that if a bullied person can avoid looking upset, then he or she is not giving the bully the response that the bully wants. The bully might try to get an upset reaction in other ways, but if the bullied person can stop himself or herself from looking upset, then the bully is likely to give up and go away, or at least go away and pick on someone else.

Even if you hurt on the inside, trying to look in control on the outside is still a good idea. You are sending the bully a message – 'You can't get to me!' There are four ways that you can use in order to avoid looking upset when being verbally bullied:

The main options are:

1   *The silent treatment.* This could include:

   (a) Avoiding the person who is bullying or harassing you altogether.

   (b) Walking away (not running away) from the bully if you see them coming.

   (c) Completely ignoring it when someone is calling you names – pretending that you haven't heard them at all.

2   *Humour.* Many professional comedians say that they started telling jokes to put bullies off from bullying them at school. I am not saying that being bullied is the way to start a career in show business! But this does show that lots of people have used humour to avoid giving the bullies the upset reaction that they want. Using humour could include:

(a)   Thinking of a witty response to the names that you are called, or the nasty things that people say to you (get some responses ready at home, for example, the bully says, 'You're stupid!', and you reply, 'Well, that makes two of us').

(b)   Acting as if it doesn't bother you, by literally laughing it off (difficult, but possible).

3   *Saying 'thanks' to everything.* This is a bit of a strange one, but it can work! When someone is verbally bullying us, and trying to get us upset, the last thing that they expect us to say is 'thanks'! This leaves the bully totally confused, but with the firm idea that they cannot get to you. One of the people who wrote this book remembers a friend of his (David) using this tactic at school. David was a bit heavier than the other students. So bullies would say things like, 'Oh, you're so fat', or 'Move out of the way, I can't see the sun', or other stupid comments that were meant to be funny. When this happened, David would reply, 'Yeah, thanks!', or, 'Cheers for that!' The bullies quickly realized that this was a person who they couldn't get to. This is because even though David was hurting inside, he still managed to make it look like it didn't bother him.

4   *Assertiveness.* Assertiveness means standing up for oneself without being aggressive or violent. When people tell you to stand up for yourself against bullies, this is what they should mean – and not physically fighting them. This is the hardest one of all, but the most effective. Here are some ideas on how to be assertive in situations where you have been verbally bullied:

(a)   Stand up straight, look confident, speak clearly and firmly, look the bully straight in the eyes, and telling the bully that you want him or her to stop.

(b)   Tell the person bullying you that you don't care what they think of you, and that calling you names isn't going to get you upset.

(c)   Tell the person bullying you that what he or she thinks will upset you doesn't bother you at all. For example:

(i)   'So what if I'm short? I don't mind it at all.'

(ii)   'So what if I wear glasses? I think they look great.'

(d)   Remembering that the bully has the problem and not you, you can ask them in a confident and calm way, 'What's your problem?'

If you are being verbally bullied, it's a good idea to practise these four types of tactics before you use them. You can do this in your imagination, with your friends or, best of all, with someone at home – just get the person at home to read this part of the book. Try to think of the worst thing that a bully could say to you – the thing that you are most afraid of hearing. See if you could use a silent, humorous, saying 'thanks' or assertive response. We think that at least one of these could work in most situations!

Please remember that if none of these help, the only way you can get the bullying to stop is by talking to an adult at school or at home.

Finally, if any young person can think of other ways to cope with verbal bullying – especially if it's something you've used yourself, and it works, and you think it could help other young people – please write to us and let us know. If you need help in writing to us, ask a teacher or an adult at home. We will be very glad to hear from you.

HOW YOU CAN HELP PREVENT BULLYING IN YOUR SCHOOL

Sometimes students feel that they don't have a lot of power within school. They feel that they simply have to obey the rules of the school, which have been set by the teachers, and that there is nothing much they can do to change things. But in the case of getting a school to be 'bully-free', students really can help! In this part of the chapter, we will be thinking about things that students can do to help prevent bullying in their schools.

Don't be a bully yourself!

This is a simple one, and in a way, the most important. Hopefully, if you've read this far, you will now agree that bullying is wrong. There is nothing good about bullying others – it is nasty and unfair. Bullying is the actions of a coward. So don't bully others, or allow your friends to bully others. If you see your friends picking on other people, tell them to stop. Remind them of how stupid and cowardly they are being, and that no one wants to be friends with a nasty bully.

Always remember that a person who is left out of things feels bullied, too; it is no fun to be on your own. Try to include people, instead of leaving them out. You never know, you might meet new friends this way, and you can never have too many friends. Remember that it's just as easy to be nice to people as it is to be nasty to people, but it's a lot more fun to be nice! In general, try to treat other people as you would like to have them treat you.

Understanding how other people feel

One of the interesting things about people is that they feel differently about different things. Another interesting thing is that people can have very strong feelings. If you put these facts together, we can realize that it is possible for John to hate something, whilst his friend James might really like exactly the same thing!

To give an example, many people in Britain and Ireland like to watch soccer. In soccer, as in other games, there are many rivalries between teams: between Manchester United and Liverpool, Arsenal and Tottenham Hotspur, Rangers and Celtic, and Heart of Midlothian and Hibernian, for example. The supporters of one team might love it when the team they support wins, and even really enjoy it when their team's big rivals lose. So, when the great soccer rivals play each other (assuming it's not a draw), the two sets of opposing supporters will feel very differently. For example, if Manchester United were to beat Liverpool one Saturday, the Manchester United supporters would look forward to seeing the Liverpool supporters at school on Monday, in order to make a bit of fun of them. The Liverpool supporters would go to school perhaps feeling that, 'Oh, I hope I don't see too many United fans today – they're bound to be feeling smug'.

But here's something interesting, and something to think about – if someone were to tell the United and Liverpool fans (or Arsenal and Spurs fans, Celtic and Rangers fans, or Hearts and Hibs fans) that soccer itself was a boring game, or a waste of time, then supporters of all the teams would stick together, and probably tell that person that soccer is a great game, and really worth watching and playing, and so on. Do remember that players who play as hard as they can against each other in league matches all year will play together in international matches!

Likewise, someone who likes a certain sort of music (let's say metal) is unlikely to want to listen to someone else's CDs if those CDs have all been recorded by boy bands.

In other words, your own feelings about things might be strong – but not every person feels the same way about things that you do. It would, in fact, be a very boring life if everyone felt the same way about things – what would we find to talk about, we wonder? Even though people feel differently about things, it is very important to try and understand how people feel. How can you ever be a good friend to someone if you don't try and understand that person's feelings? If everyone was to try and understand how other people feel, we wouldn't have so many problems in life.

If you are ever tempted to pick on someone, or to join in bullying someone, think about how a person feels when he or she has been bullied. Think about whether you would like to feel that way. Then you will realize, we hope, that picking on or bullying someone is not something that you should do.

Respecting other people for who they are

As we've seen, people are different in how they feel about things. But people are different in other ways, too. When we meet a person for the first time, particularly if that person is from another place, or looks somehow different on the outside to us, sometimes that person can seem strange. We have to accept that people are different, and respect those differences. But it is very important to try and look for similarities you have with other people, rather than thinking about the differences only. Don't judge other people, or listen to those who judge others. And remember, never treat people badly because of their race, religion, nationality, sexuality or any aspect of their appearance.

Dealing with your own feelings

We have found that many young people get involved in bullying, and in fights and arguments in general, because they don't control their own anger, or find it difficult to do so. Sometimes this means that the young person will end up in trouble at school. Everybody gets angry sometimes, of course. But the problems start when we get angry at one thing, and take our anger out on another person. Sometimes people who bully are angry at something that has happened at home (say, their parents arguing) or school (a teacher who they think has treated them unfairly). What happens is that they store up all this anger inside them, and take this anger out on a 'safe target' – someone who won't or can't fight back.

There are, of course, those who don't take their anger out on others, but bottle it up inside themselves. This can result in strong feelings of frustration and hatred, and can lead the person to want to hurt or even kill themselves. Because of this, it is important to share your feelings and the reasons for your strong emotions with others.

Because of these reasons, we think that it is important for young people to learn a bit about anger and how they can deal with it. So here are some things to think about:

- *What does anger feel like?* When we get angry, things happen inside our body. Our heart beat gets faster; our breathing gets heavier and faster; our muscles tense up; we feel 'butterflies' in our stomach; our blood pumps around our body faster (this is why we get red in the face); we feel hot and bothered, and sometimes (if we are really angry) ready to 'explode'. You can learn to recognize these things as 'warning signs' from your body. If you begin to feel this way, and something is annoying you, then it's time to try to calm yourself down!

- *How do we behave when we are angry?* People behave in different ways when they are angry. One person might scream or shout; another might cry (tears of rage and frustration, not tears of sadness); another might go completely silent. Think about what you do – what's your anger style?

- *What makes us angry?* We have already seen how people feel differently about different things. So it should be no surprise to find out that different things make different people angry. Anger can also result from feeling frustrated, embarrassed or afraid. Think about what makes you angry. Make a list. If your anger is getting you into trouble, can you avoid those things, or think about them in a different way?

- *What alternatives do we have to being angry? How do we calm ourselves down?* There are lots of different ways to cope with angry feelings. You will have to pick the way that is right for you. Some people will do something as simple as counting to ten in their own heads. This stops them in their tracks, and gives them a chance to calm down and take control of themselves. Some people like to think about something else – something happy, peaceful, or something that they enjoy doing – in order to stop themselves thinking about whatever is making them angry. Other people will deliberately start a conversation, or join in another conversation, that is about a subject other than what is making them angry. Still other people find it helpful to talk to someone they trust about their angry feelings, in order to express these feelings in a safe way, without hurting anyone else. Finally, some people find that it is helpful to 'get the energy out of their system' by playing a sport, or doing some exercise (this is a good one). If you have problems controlling your anger, and especially if this has got you into trouble in the past, you should try and find a set of ways to cope from the things we have suggested. Remember, different ways to cope will help in different situations.

Talk to your friends, teachers and the people who look after you at home about these ideas. The more ideas you have for coping with anger, the better. And the better we are able to cope with angry feelings, the less likely we are to pick on or join in bullying others.

Other things to do in school

We have just looked at a few things that students can do themselves to help prevent bullying in their schools. There are many other things that students can do in school, and in lessons, with the help of the school staff, in order to prevent bullying in schools. Some of this 'anti-bullying work' is actually a lot of fun. If you would like to do this, talk to your teacher, and ask them to read this book.

SUMMARY

- In the first main part of this chapter, 'What every young person needs to know about bullying', we first looked at what bullying is and the different types of bullying.

- In the second main part of this chapter, 'What to do if you are being bullied', we advised that if you are being bullied that you must tell an adult you trust, to remember that the bully has the problem, not you, and not to fight back physically. We also talked about some things you can do about being verbally bullied.

- In the last main part of this chapter, 'How you can help prevent bullying in your school', we said that students really can help in creating a 'bully-free' school – don't bully others, or allow your friends to bully others; try to understand how other people feel and respect other people for who they are. We also suggested some ways in which young people can think about and learn to cope with angry feelings, and said that there are many other things that students can do in school, and in lessons, in order to prevent bullying in schools.

FURTHER RESOURCES FOR YOUNG PEOPLE

Elliott, M. (1999) *The Bully Wise Guide*. London: Hodder.

Johnson, J. (1996) *How Do I Feel about Bullies and Gangs?* London: Aladdin Books.

Stones, R. (1998) *Don't Pick On Me: How to Handle Bullying*. London: Piccadilly Press.

A final word

At this point, what remains to say? Simply this – we want school communities to be free of bullying behaviour. As professionals within the field of education, and as members of school communities, this would be the optimal outcome, and what we feel could be the most solid contribution that we can make towards a society that is similarly free of physical and psychological violence.

Is this just a pipe dream? Hopefully not. As human beings, we are responsible for the society in which we live. We cannot say that we are 'not involved' or that it is 'nothing to do with us'. Human beings are capable of choices.

This is why we felt that adults in all possible bullying situations must intervene. If we fail to do so, then we must think about whom we are failing. As well as this failing in our duty of care to our young people, we should also think about what else has been lost on a broader scale when we fail to intervene in situations of bullying behaviour.

Many parents and those who work with young people in educational settings are concerned as to the effect that the media has on young people's attitudes and behaviour. Do violent films cause violent behaviour? Young people are certainly more exposed to anti-social, pro-violence messages from films, television, books and magazines, computer games and the Internet than ever before, and this increasing exposure unfortunately looks set to continue.

As Nelson Mandela said in his Foreword to the *World Report on Violence and Health* (World Health Organisation, 2002), 'We owe it to our children – the most vulnerable citizens in society – a life free from violence and fear'. In order to achieve this everyone must, as Mandela said, 'be tireless in our efforts' to attain a non-violent society. So what better place to start than in the school and home?

If this book has provided some ideas for concrete ways in which members of school communities can, in collaboration, intervene against bullying and aggressive behaviour in schools, then we will have succeeded in our aims.

In different parts of the book, we have encouraged readers to contact us, should they have some additional insight into the issues that we describe, or perhaps have experiences or knowledge that may serve to illuminate and address weaknesses in the text. This is not a mere pretence at academic humility, but rather a genuine request. The authors of this book, and the team with which they work, may be contacted via the following details:

The Anti-Bullying Research and Resource Centre

Department of Education

Trinity College Dublin

Republic of Ireland

Tel/Fax: + 353 1 608 2573

This is the end of our book on practical anti-bullying work. But in reality, all that has been achieved is the marking off of territory and the discussion of tactics for another fresh beginning in this work.

Mona O' Moore

Stephen James Minton

Dublin, 2004

Photocopiable resources

All these photocopiable resources are available to download from the PCP website: **http://www.paulchapmanpublishing.co.uk/pcp/resources/pcp resource.aspx.**

 **APPENDIX A: RESOURCES FOR TALKS/TRAINING WITH SCHOOL MANAGEMENT STAFF**

CHAPTER 2

BULLYING, AGGRESSIVE
BEHAVIOUR AND HARASSMENT
AMONGST YOUNG PEOPLE IN
SCHOOLS: WHAT SCHOOL
MANAGEMENT STAFF NEED TO KNOW

CHAPTER 2

Topics of Discussion

- 1 – What is School Bullying?
- 2 – Types of Bullying
- 3A – Formulating Effective Anti-Bullying Policy in Schools (1): Issues to be Aware of
- 3B – Formulating Effective Anti-Bullying Policy in Schools (2): Consultation and Collaboration with the School Community
- 3C – Formulating Effective Anti-Bullying Policy in Schools (3): Establishing Measures for Dissemination, Promotion and Evaluation
- 4A – Formulating Effective Anti-Bullying Strategies in Schools: Countering Strategies (1): Specifying how incidents of alleged bullying behaviour are to be reported, investigated and recorded (1)
- 4B – Formulating Effective Anti-Bullying Strategies in Schools: Countering Strategies (2): Specifying how incidents of alleged bullying behaviour are to be reported, investigated and recorded (2)
- 4C – Formulating Effective Anti-Bullying Strategies in Schools (3): Countering Strategies (3): Specifying how incidents of alleged bullying behaviour are to be reported, investigated and recorded (3)
- 4D – Formulating Effective Anti-Bullying Strategies in Schools (4): Preventative Strategies
- 5 – Questions and Answers

CHAPTER 2

1 – What is School Bullying?

- '…. the systematic abuse of power' (Smith and Sharp, 1994).

- 'Bullying is long-standing violence, mental or physical, conducted by an individual or a group against an individual who is not able to defend himself or herself in that actual situation' (Roland, 1989, in Mellor, 1999).

CHAPTER 2

2 – Types of Bullying

- Direct Bullying
  - Verbal Bullying
  - Physical Bullying
  - Gesture Bullying
  - Extortion
  - E-Bullying
- Indirect Bullying

- Girls and boys tend to be involved to differing extents in the various types of bullying behaviour.
- Labelling someone as a 'bully' is not helpful. Instead of using the 'blame/ punishment' approach, we advocate the *'no blame'* approach: challenging and changing the inappropriate behaviour.
- Young people who are involved in bullying, aggressive behaviour and harassment as either victims or perpetrators (or in some cases, both), need the help and intervention of both parents and school personnel.
- Bullying is best viewed as a *community issue* – don't focus exclusively on the student-student dyad, but consider also teacher-on-student, student-on-teacher, and parent-on-teacher (etc.).

CHAPTER 2

3A – Formulating Effective Anti-Bullying Policy in Schools (1)

- Issues to be aware of
  - Who will take the *responsibility* for the formation and implementation of anti-bullying policy and strategies?
  - What are the *overall goals* for the anti-bullying policy?
  - Should we focus *exclusively on bullying*, or cover related issues such as aggressive behaviour, harassment, or indiscipline?
  - Who should this policy *serve*? Students? Teachers? Everyone?
  - How can we find practical ways of *involving classroom staff, parents* and *students* in the policy formation process?
  - What are the relevant *legal, curricular* and *policy issues* to be aware of?

CHAPTER 2

3B – Formulating Effective Anti-Bullying Policy in Schools (2)

- Consultation and Collaboration with the School Community
  - In order for people to feel ownership over a policy directive, they need to have been consulted
  - To be arranged:
    - classroom staff in-service training;
    - evening talks/open days with parents/community members;
    - classroom work with students
  - All groups need input on:
    - what bullying is, and the forms it takes;
    - the 'no blame' philosophy and approach;
    - conceptualizing bullying behaviour as a community issue
    - ideas around investigating, recording, countering and preventing bullying behaviour
  - Note – these groups will have different levels of knowledge, beliefs, feelings and concerns about bullying behaviour

CHAPTER 2

3C – Formulating Effective Anti-Bullying Policy in Schools (3)

- Establishing Measures for Dissemination, Promotion and Evaluation
  - A school should be proud of its proactive stance against bullying
  - The written anti-bullying statement should be:
    - Construed as a matter of *public record*
    - Displayed on school notice boards as a *permanent poster*
    - Available to all school *students* in a language they can understand
    - Given to all members of *staff*, especially *new* and *non-permanent members*
    - Given to all *parents*, especially those *'new'* to the school
    - Distributed to all *relevant groups* in the *school community*
    - *Evaluation* and *review measures* should be 'built in' – reviews must be made at least annually

CHAPTER 2

4A – Formulating Effective Anti-Bullying Strategies in Schools (1)

- Countering Strategies (1)
  - Specifying how incidents of alleged bullying behaviour are to be reported, investigated and recorded (1)
    - Can be enormous social pressure against reporting
    - Co-ordination of anti-bullying countering strategies
    - Talks to the whole student body
    - The essentials of reporting procedures
      - Attend to the person's *safety* needs; the victim needs to be safeguarded from future incidents of bullying behaviour, esp. acts of retribution
      - Communicate *acceptance* of what the person says
      - Listen actively, don't interpret, record specific grievances (esp. re: concrete events)
      - Consider use of *standardized reporting forms*

CHAPTER 2

4B – Formulating Effective Anti-Bullying Strategies in Schools (2)

- Countering Strategies (2)
  - Specifying how incidents of alleged bullying behaviour are to be reported, investigated and recorded (2)
    - Talks/interviews with those involved in bullying
      - Alleged perpetrators and victims to be interviewed separately
      - Where a gang is involved, interview members separately in the first instance
      - It is advisable to investigate as soon as is possible
      - It is extremely helpful to talk to witnesses to the event
      - An accusatory tone is not helpful: assure alleged perpetrator that his or her side will be heard before a decision is made
      - It is not necessary to tell the alleged perpetrator who has reported the incident – only that the incident has come to the attention of the school authorities, and that bullying behaviour is not tolerated in the school

CHAPTER 2

4C – Formulating Effective Anti-Bullying Strategies in Schools (3)

- Countering Strategies (3)
  - Specifying how incidents of alleged bullying behaviour are to be reported, investigated and recorded (3)
    - After investigation, perpetrators of bullying should be informed (in good faith):
      - That his or her behaviour constituted an unambiguous incident of bullying behaviour, and that this contravenes school policy;
      - He or she must refrain from bullying, and the particular forms of bullying behaviour experienced by the victim, in future;
      - That specified sanction, in line with the anti-bullying policy, will be implemented if future instances occur;
      - That acts of retribution against the victim will be dealt with by the severest possible applications of these sanctions
  - The Role of Parents
  - Specifying Sanctions for those Involved as Perpetrators
    - Consider use of standardized *written behavioural contracts*

CHAPTER 2

4D – Formulating Effective Anti-Bullying Strategies in Schools (4)

- Preventative Strategies
  - Specifying Support Systems for those Involved
    - Consider use of mediation, mentorship schemes, social skills training, counselling services and:
  - Classroom Awareness Work with Students
    - Can be promoted to teachers through classroom staff in-service training
    - May include creative work (art, drama, sculpture, etc.), analysis of books and poetry, structured discussion, 'circle time', and (esp.) the use of class charters
    - Important to put students' work on public display
    - Important to students' input apropos all aspects of school anti-bullying policy and strategy
  - Peer Mediation and Peer Mentorship and their Role

CHAPTER 2

THANKS FOR LISTENING!

ANY QUESTIONS?

APPENDIX B: RESOURCES FOR TALKS/TRAINING WITH CLASSROOM STAFF

CHAPTER 3

BULLYING, AGGRESSIVE
BEHAVIOUR AND HARASSMENT
AMONGST YOUNG PEOPLE IN
SCHOOLS: WHAT CLASSROOM STAFF
NEED TO KNOW

CHAPTER 3

Topics of Discussion

- 1 - What is School Bullying?
- 2 - Types of Bullying
- 3 – Further Key Issues for Classroom Staff
- 4A – Dealing with Incidents of Bullying Behaviour (1): Conflict Resolution and Conflict Management
- 4B – Dealing with Incidents of Bullying Behaviour (2): Support Strategies for those involved in Bullying Behaviour
- 5A – Preventative Strategies (1): General Talks to Class Groups about Bullying Behaviour
- 5B – Preventative Strategies (2): Specific Anti-Bullying Activity Classes
- 5C – Preventative Strategies (3): Anti-Bullying Across the Curriculum
- 6 – Questions and Answers

CHAPTER 3

1 - What is School Bullying?

- '…. the systematic abuse of power' (Smith and Sharp, 1994).

- 'Bullying is long-standing violence, mental or physical, conducted by an individual or a group against an individual who is not able to defend himself or herself in that actual situation' (Roland, 1989, in Mellor, 1999).

CHAPTER 3

2 - Types of Bullying

- Direct Bullying
  - Verbal Bullying
  - Physical Bullying
  - Gesture Bullying
  - Extortion
  - E-Bullying
- Indirect Bullying

- Girls and boys tend to be involved to differing extents in the various types of bullying behaviour.
- Labelling someone as a 'bully' is not helpful. Instead of using the 'blame / punishment' approach, we advocate the *'no blame'* approach: challenging and changing the inappropriate behaviour.
- Young people who are involved in bullying, aggressive behaviour and harassment as either victims or perpetrators (or in some cases, both), need the help and intervention of both parents and school personnel.
- Bullying is best viewed as a *community issue* – don't focu exclusively on the student-student dyad, but consider also teacher-on-student, student-on-teacher, and parent-on-teacher (etc).

CHAPTER 3

3 – Further Key Issues for Classroom Staff

- Anti-Bullying Policy in Schools
  - Should specify:
    - How bullying is defined, and the forms it takes
    - How incidents of alleged bullying behaviour are to be reported, investigated and recorded
    - How incidents of bullying behaviour are to be dealt with, including support and intervention strategies for those involved (both perpetrators and victims) and, where necessary, the specification of sanctions for perpetrators
    - Preventative strategies in the school and classroom
    - The role of school management staff, classroom staff, parents / guardians, students and relevant others in the above
    - Measures for dissemination, evaluation and review
  - Should underpin all of the anti-bullying work that is undertaken in schools
- The Role of Classroom Staff in Anti-Bullying Work
  - The practical and day-to-day implementation of the procedures and strategies specified in the school's anti-bullying policy

CHAPTER 3

4A – Dealing with Incidents of Bullying Behaviour (1)

- Conflict Resolution and Conflict Management
  - A five-stage model
    - Identification, assessment, formulation of causes, intervention, evaluation
  - Being objective, and being perceived as being so
    - Equal and fair consideration to each side before action; action will be fair and just, and be a consequence of the choices made by the people involved in the conflict, and their subsequent behaviour
    - Ground rules and taking notes
  - Dealing with feelings
    - People rarely fight about facts or events, but rather how they feel about them
    - Attending to safety needs, use of active listening, open-ended and feeling-level questions, empathic standpoint
- Conflict Management
  - Where compromise is *not* possible – enter into a third-party arbitrated agreement
  - Hopefully, paves the way for future conflict resolution
- N.B. - Bullying may *not* involve conflict (*mutual* antagonism / dislike / distrust), but may be connected to the perpetrator's desire to manipulate and exert power

CHAPTER 3

4B – Dealing with Incidents of Bullying Behaviour (2)

- Support Strategies for those Involved in Bullying Behaviour
  - Counselling / emotional support services for those who have been victimised
    - Undertaken by a suitably qualified professional
    - Should be just one of a range of options
  - Social skills work
    - Anti-social persistent perpetrators
    - 'Provocative' victims
    - Can be undertaken by skilled classroom staff member or suitably qualified professional
  - Emotional (esp. *anger*) management work
    - 'Unintentional' perpetrators, or those poor in impulse control
    - Can be undertaken by skilled classroom staff member or suitably qualified professional

CHAPTER 3

5A – Preventative Strategies (1)

- General Talks to Class Groups about Bullying Behaviour
  - Key points to put across:
    - what bullying is, and the different forms that it can take;
    - that bullying is, and is seen in this school, as an unacceptable form of behaviour;
    - that we all have a responsibility to safeguard the well-being of others;
    - that if we are being bullied, or if we know about someone else being bullied, that the best way to get help is to tell a member of school staff;
    - that violent retaliation will only make things worse in the long run;
    - that everyone has a right to a school that is free of bullying and harassment, and we all have to play our part in achieving this.
  - Repetition is essential; a guideline could be that young people in school should hear such a talk at least once a term

CHAPTER 3

5B – Preventative Strategies (2)
- Specific Anti-Bullying Activity Classes
  - General points
    - Whole class groups with a self-esteem focus; inclusiveness
    - Combination of creative media and facilitated discussion work
    - 'Circle time': group work and group boundaries
  - Warm-up activities
  - Video and structured discussion sessions
  - Visual arts
    - Posters, pictures and sculpture
  - Performance arts
    - Musical composition and drama sessions
    - Role-play and its problems
  - The use of class charters
  - Public display of students' creative contributions

CHAPTER 3

5C – Preventative Strategies (3)

- Anti-Bullying Across the Curriculum
  - It is possible to convey an anti-bullying message through one's day-to-day teaching practise
  - Primary teachers have perhaps a greater degree of freedom over curriculum, but this is possible in subject teaching at the secondary school level, too
  - General advice – take the issue of bullying behaviour in schools seriously, and then take every opportunity, using one's own creativity and ingenuity to convey a pro-social and anti-bullying message

CHAPTER 3

THANKS FOR LISTENING!

ANY QUESTIONS?

APPENDIX C: RESOURCES FOR TALKS WITH PARENTS

CHAPTER 4

BULLYING, AGGRESSIVE
BEHAVIOUR AND HARASSMENT
AMONGST YOUNG PEOPLE IN
SCHOOLS: WHAT PARENTS NEED TO
KNOW

CHAPTER 4

Topics of Discussion

- 1 - What is School Bullying?
- 2 - Types of Bullying
- 3 - Why Parents are so Important
- 4 - Signs and Symptoms of Being Bullied
- 5 - What To Do If Your Child / Teenager Is Being Bullied
- 6 - What To Do If Your Child / Teenager Is Bullying Others
- 7A - Working With Your Child's / Teenager's School Against Bullying (1): What you and your child / teenager will want and need to know
- 7B - Working With Your Child's / Teenager's School Against Bullying (2): Parent-school collaboration against bullying behaviour
- 8 – Questions and Answers

CHAPTER 4

1 - What is School Bullying?

- Bullying is a form of aggressive behaviour that is conducted by a young person or group of young people, on a systematic and ongoing basis, against a young person who is singled out, and is relatively unable to defend himself or herself. It is not bullying, for instance, when young people of around the same age and level of physical / social power have the occasional fight or quarrel.

CHAPTER 4

2 - Types of Bullying

- Direct Bullying
  - Verbal Bullying
  - Physical Bullying
  - Gesture Bullying
  - Extortion
  - E-Bullying
- Indirect Bullying

- Girls and boys tend to be involved to differing extents in the various types of bullying behaviour.
- Labelling someone as a 'bully' is not helpful. Instead of using the 'blame / punishment' approach, we advocate challenging and changing the inappropriate behaviour.
- Young people who are involved in bullying, aggressive behaviour and harassment as either victims or perpetrators (or in some cases, both), need the help and intervention of both parents and school personnel.

CHAPTER 4

3 - Why Parents are so Important

- Parents are the biggest single influence on their children's attitudes and behaviour.
- Every responsible parent is concerned for the protection, safety and well-being of his or her child / teenager.
- Along with school personnel, parents have a responsibility to ensure that their children / teenagers are not involved in bullying or harassing other school students.
- Research shows that bullied young people are reluctant to tell their parents or their teachers that they have been bullied at school. However, when they do tell someone, they are more likely to tell their parents than their teachers.

CHAPTER 4

4 - Signs and Symptoms of Being Bullied

- The young person looks distressed or anxious, and yet refuses to say what is wrong
- Unexplained cuts and bruises
- Damage to clothes, books, and school equipment
- Doing worse at school than before
- Requests for extra money
- Reluctance to go to school
- Changes in mood and behaviour
- Lacking in confidence or self-esteem
- Complaints of headaches and stomach aches
- Problems sleeping

Unfortunately, this is not a fail-proof checklist. The presence of some of these things, or even all of them, doesn't necessarily mean that the young person is being bullied. However, if these signs and symptoms persist, parents should investigate the matter further.

CHAPTER 4

5 - What To Do If Your Child / Teenager Is Being Bullied

- Finding out what's wrong
  - It is not easy for young people to tell their parents that they have been victimised.
  - Let the young person know that you are there for him or her
  - Be prepared to both listen and talk, but to listen more!
- Reassure your child / teenager that the bully has the problem
- Tell them not to fight back physically!
- Teaching coping skills
  - Explain to the bullied young person that bullies want an upset reaction Humour, silence, or an assertive response – i.e., standing up for oneself in a non-aggressive way – may well prevent a further attack
  - Teaching coping skills at home
- The Importance of Self-Esteem
  - Young people who are bullied can so easily lose their confidence, which will affect their sense of self-worth. The more often one is bullied, the lower will be the level of one's self-esteem
  - Ideas for building self-esteem at home
- Reporting the Problem (see slide 7A)

CHAPTER 4

6 - What To Do If Your Child / Teenager Is Bullying Others

- Awareness of what bullying is
- Be a good role model
- Finding out what's wrong
- The importance of self-esteem
  - Perpetrators of bullying have lowered levels of self-esteem; the more often one bullies others, the lower is one's level of self-esteem.
  - Bullying others can, then, be seen as a misguided attempt to gain self-esteem (perhaps in the form of peer recognition)
  - Some young people are involved in bullying behaviour as both perpetrators and victims (bully-victims) – they have the lowest levels of self-esteem of all
- Teaching empathy at home
- Teaching respect for differences at home
- Letting off steam in a positive way

CHAPTER 4

7A - Working With Your Child's / Teenager's School Against Bullying (1)

- What you and your child / teenager will want and need to know
  - The young person may beg or plead with the parent not to tell
  - Sometimes the young person needs to be over-ruled, but we have to be sure that what we are doing really is in his or her best interests
  - We must be sure that the school can and will handle the matter in a sensitive and responsible way
    - The incident will be treated in a sensitive manner, and that confidentiality will be kept as far as is possible
    - Your child / teenager will be safeguarded, as far as it is possible, against further incidents of bullying behaviour
    - You as a parent will be kept informed about the progress of this case
  - Parents should of course be aware that investigating an allegation of bullying behaviour in a sensitive and thorough manner may well be time consuming

CHAPTER 4

7B - Working With Your Child's / Teenager's School Against Bullying (2)

- Parent-school collaboration against bullying behaviour
  - Many schools have a Parents' Council, or Parents'-Teachers' Association
  - Parents should be consulted on matters of school planning, and the drafting of new or revised school policy / codes
  - Parents' organisations can themselves fund and source guest speakers for information evenings, and co-fund or partake in ongoing preventative measures against bullying behaviour – 'Anti-Bullying Weeks', and so on
  - Parents can, and indeed should, organise themselves if necessary, to ensure that their local communities are 'bully-free'.
  - Teachers and parents should be on the 'same side of the fence': an alliance of responsible, caring adults with the common aim of preventing and countering bullying, aggressive behaviour and harassment amongst young people in schools

CHAPTER 4

THANKS FOR LISTENING!

ANY QUESTIONS?

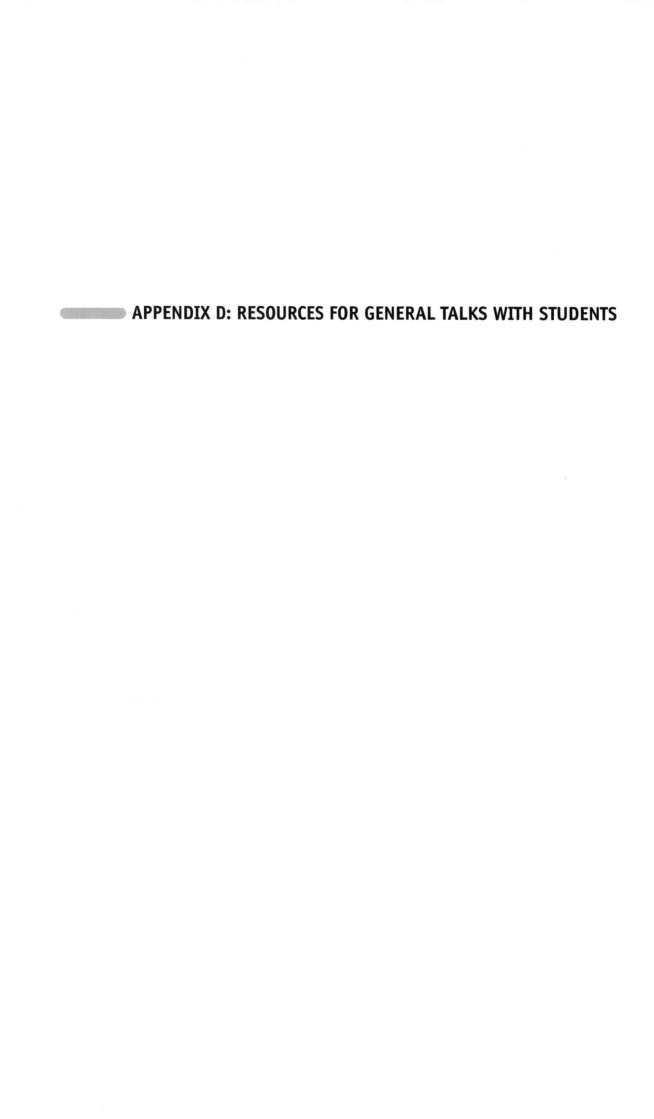

APPENDIX D: RESOURCES FOR GENERAL TALKS WITH STUDENTS

CHAPTER 5

BULLYING IN SCHOOLS: WHAT YOUNG PEOPLE NEED TO KNOW

CHAPTER 5

Things to Discuss

- **1 - What Every Young Person Needs to Know About Bullying**
- **2 - What to Do if You are Being Bullied**
- **3 - How to Help Prevent Bullying in Your School**
- **4 - Questions and Answers**

CHAPTER 5

1 - What Every Young Person Needs to Know About Bullying

- What is Bullying?
  - We say that a student is being bullied when he or she is *singled out* in an *unpleasant way* by another student *or* group of students. The bullied student is *picked on again and again*, and it is *difficult* for him or her to defend himself or herself
  - It's NOT bullying when people of about the same age and power have the occasional fight or quarrel
  - It is NOT bullying when a teacher acts on the school rules, or offers fair criticism of a student's work
- The Different Types of Bullying
  - *Verbal* Bullying: name-calling, cruel teasing, slagging, threatening
  - *Physical* Bullying: hitting, kicking, hurting in some way
  - *Gesture* Bullying: threatening or offensive gestures
  - *Extortion*: taking money, possessions or equipment from somebody
  - *Isolation*: leaving someone out all of the time, sometimes by spreading rumours, lies or gossip in order to make others not like the bullied person
  - *E-Bullying*: nasty e-mail or text messages
- Can you think of any more?

CHAPTER 5

2A - What to Do if You are Being Bullied (I)

- **Talking to Adults About Being Bullied – Why it's So Important, and How to Do It**
- Nobody can help you unless you let them know
- By helping yourself, you are helping others too
- There's nothing wrong in telling an adult that you or someone else has been bullied
  - People in this situation sometimes get called a 'tell-tale', or even worse names, but this is WRONG
  - If you tell a tale just to get someone into trouble, this is not a nice thing
  - If you tell someone you've been bullied, this is different. You are telling because you want the bullying to stop. If the bully ends up in trouble, this is because he was doing something very wrong in the first place
  - It can help to talk to a parent or guardian first – they will be able to find out from the school how the school will handle it

CHAPTER 5

2B - What to Do if You are Being Bullied (II)

- Remember, the Bully has the Problem, Not You
  - Bullies and their friends are very good at getting the people they bully to believe that there is 'something the matter' with them
  - Remember, people can be bullied 'for' a number of so-called 'reasons', which are really just excuses to behave in a nasty way
  - There is NO excuse or reason to bully someone!
- Don't Fight Back Physically!
  - We are often told that we should stand up for ourselves and physically fight bullies, but this is WRONG
  - If we lose:
    - we will be beaten up even worse
  - If we win (very unlikely):
    - Either, the bully could pretend that he or she was the one who was picked on, and we will be in trouble with the school, or
    - The bully will get his or her friends and relations to take revenge
  - If we get together a gang, or something like that:
    - the bully gets together a *bigger* gang, so then we get an *even bigger* gang, then the bully gets an *even bigger gang than that*…. and sooner or later, someone ends up in hospital / expelled / in trouble with the police

---

CHAPTER 5

2C – What to Do if You are Being Bullied (III)

- How to Cope if You are Being Verbally Bullied
  - Remember, if you have been *physically* hurt, the school or police should deal with this, but you can do something yourself about *verbal* bullying
  - Remember, bullies want an *upset* reaction
  - If we can *avoid* giving an upset reaction, then we buy ourselves some time
  - Try one of *four tactics*:
    - The silent treatment
    - Use of humour
    - Saying 'thanks' to everything
    - Assertiveness – standing up for yourself in a non-aggressive way

---

CHAPTER 5

3A – How to Help Prevent Bullying in Your School (I)

- Don't Be A Bully Yourself!
  - There's nothing good about bullying others – it is WRONG, and bullying is the actions of a COWARD
  - Don't pick on others, or let your friends pick on others
  - Try to include people instead of leaving them out
  - Treat other people how you would like to be treated yourself
- Understanding How Other People Feel
  - Not everybody feels the same way you do about everything!
  - It's hard to understand how others feel, but it is worth it
  - Think – how do people feel when they are being bullied?
- Respecting Other People For Who They Are
  - Think about what you have in common with a person, instead of thinking about the differences
  - Don't judge people, or listen to others who judge people
  - Don't treat people badly because of their race, religion, sexuality or nationality

---

CHAPTER 5

3B - How to Help Prevent Bullying in Your School (II)

- Dealing With Your Own Feelings
  - Many people bully others, or get in trouble in other ways, because they don't control their *anger*
  - Questions to think about:
    - What does anger feel like?
    - How do we behave when we are angry?
    - What things make each of us angry?
    - Has anger got us into trouble before?
    - What alternatives do we have to losing our temper?
    - How can we calm ourselves down?

CHAPTER 5

CHAPTER 5

3C – How to Help Prevent Bullying in Your School (III)

- **Other Things to Do in School**
  - Always play fair in classes, sports, activities, and out of school
  - Treat others how you'd like to be treated yourself
  - Ask your teachers if you can do some anti-bullying work, or have an 'anti-bullying week'
  - Get involved in mediation/mentoring/ prefecting where these things exist
  - Make a class charter

THANKS FOR LISTENING!

ANY QUESTIONS?

Notes

CHAPTER 1

1 Amongst other places, documented in Olweus, D. (1993) *Bullying: What We Know and What We Can Do*. Oxford: Blackwell.
2 O'Moore, A.M., Kirkham, C. and Smith, M. (1997) 'Bullying behaviour in Irish schools: a nationwide study', *Irish Journal of Psychology*, 18 (2): 141–69.
3 Smith, P.K. (1997) 'Bullying in schools: the UK experience and the Sheffield anti-bullying project', *Irish Journal of Psychology*, 18 (2): 191–201.
4 Mellor, A. (1990). *Spotlight 23: Bullying in Scottish Secondary Schools*. Edinburgh: Scottish Council for Research in Education.
5 Rigby, K. and Slee, P.T. (1999) 'Australia' in P.K. Smith, Y. Morita, J. Junger-Tas, D. Olweus, R. Catalano and P. Slee (eds), *The Nature of School Bullying: A Cross-National Perspective*. London: Routledge.
6 Marr, N. and Field, T. (2001) *Bullycide: Death at Playtime*. Oxford: Success Unlimited.

CHAPTER 2

1 In Olweus, D. 1991 'Bully/victim problems among school children: basic facts and effects of a school based intervention program', in D. Pepler and K. Rubin (eds), *The Development and Treatment of Childhood Aggression*. Hillsdale, NJ: Lawrence Erlbaum Associates. p. 413.
2 Smith, P.K. and Sharp, S. (eds) (1998) *School Bullying: Insights and Perspectives*. London: Routledge. p. 2.
3 An acknowledged adoption of a Scandinavian definition (Roland, 1989), used in a study by Andrew Mellor (1990); cited in Mellor, A. (1999), in P.K. Smith et al. (eds), *The Nature of School Bullying: A Cross-National Perspective*. London: Routledge. pp.93–4.
4 From the Depatment of Education (1993) *Guidelines on Countering Bullying Behaviour in Primary and Post-primary Schools*. Dublin: The Stationery Office.
5 In Smith, P.K. and Thompson, D. (1991) *Practical Approaches to Bullying*. London: David Fulton.
6 This has been found to be the case in large-scale studies (for example, in Norway, Sweden, England, Scotland and the Republic of Ireland) of bullying behaviour in schools. See Smith, P.K. et al. (eds) (1999) *The Nature of School Bullying: A Cross-National Perspective*. London: Routledge Smith, P.K. (ed.) (2003) *Violence in Schools: The Response in Europe*. London: Routledge-Falmer for overviews.
7 The interested reader is recommended to refer to Robinson, G. and Maines, B. (1997) *Crying for Help: the No Blame Approach to Bullying*. Bristol: Lucky Duck.
8 See O'Moore, A.M. and Minton, S.J. (2003) 'The hidden voice of bullying' in M. Shevlin and R. Rose (eds), *Encouraging Voices: Respecting the Insights of Young People Who Have Been Marginalised*. Dublin: National Disability Authority
9 See Pikas, A. (1975) 'Treatment of mobbing in school: principles for and the results of the work of an anti-mobbing group', *Scandinavian Journal of Educational Research*, 19: 1–12.

CHAPTER 4

1 For example, Whitney and Smith's 1993 study in Sheffield, England – see Smith, P.K. and Sharp, S. (eds) (1994) *School Bullying: Insights and Perspectives*. London: Routledge; O'Moore's nationwide survey in the Republic of Ireland – see O'Moore, A.M., Kirkham, C. and Smith, M. (1997) 'Bullying behaviour in Irish schools: a nationwide study', *Irish Journal of Psychology*, 18 (2): 141–69.

2 Ibid.

3 Quoted in Sullivan, K. (1999) 'Aotearoa/New Zealand', in P.K. Smith, Y. Morita, J. Junger-Tas, D. Olweus, R. and Catalano and P. Slee (eds), *The Nature of School Bullying: A Cross-National Perspective*. London: Routledge.

4 Findings drawn from O'Moore, A.M. and Kirkham, C. (2001) 'Self-esteem and its relationship to bullying behaviour', *Aggressive Behaviour*, 27: 269–83.

5 Ibid.

Useful resources

The following comprises a list of resources (books, Internet, resource packs and videos) that we believe might be helpful in anti-bullying work in schools.

BOOKS

Textbooks and resource books for school staff, parents and other adults in the school community

Asher, S.R. and Coie, J.D. (1992) *Peer Rejection in Childhood*. Cambridge: Cambridge University Press.

Beane, A.L. (1999) *Bully Free Classroom: Over 100 Tips and Strategies for Teachers*. Minneapolis: Free Spirit.

Besag, V.E. (1994) *Bullies and Victims in Schools*. Buckingham: Open University Press.

Blagg, N. (1990) *School Phobia and its Treatment*. London: Routledge.

Blatchford, P. (1993) *Playtime in the Primary School*. London: Routledge.

Byrne, B. (1993) *Coping with Bullying in Schools*. Dublin: Columba Press.

Byrne, B. (1996) *Bullying: A Community Approach*. Dublin: Columba Press.

Cattanach, A. (1995) *Play Therapy with Abused Children*. London: Jessica Kingsley.

Cowie, H. and Wallace, P. (2000) *Peer Support in Action: From Bystanders to Standing By*. London: Sage Publications.

Dore, S. (2000) *Bullying*. NSPCC: Egmont World.

Elliot, M. (1994) *Keeping Safe: A Practical Guide to Talking with Children*. London: Coronet Books.

Elliot, M. (1996) *501 Ways to be a Good Parent*. London: Hodder & Stoughton.

Elliot, M. (1997) *101 Ways to Deal with Bullying: A Guide for Parents*. London: Hodder & Stoughton.

Elliot, M. and Shenton, G. (1999) *Bully-free: Activities to Promote Confidence and Friendship*. London: Kidscape.

Fried, S. and Fried, P. (1996) *Bullies and Victims*. New York: M. Evans.

Fried, S. and Fried, P. (2003) *Bullies, Targets and Witnesses*. New York: M. Evans.

Frude, N. and Gault, H. (1984) *Disruptive Behaviour in Schools*. New York: John Wiley.

Humphreys, T. (1993) *Self-Esteem: The Key to Your Child's Education*. Leadington, Co. Cork: T. Humphreys.

Johnston, J. (1996) *Dealing with Bullying*. New York: Rosen.

Jones, N. and Jones, E.B. (1992) *Learning to Behave*. London: Kogan Page.

La Fontaine, J. (1991) *Bullying: A Child's View*. London: Calouste Gulbenkian Foundation.

Lane, D.A. (1990) *The Impossible Child*. Stoke-on-Trent: Trentham Books.

Lee, C. (2004) *Preventing Bullying in Schools*. London: Paul Chapman Publishing.

Marr, N. and Field, T. (2001) *Bullycide: Death at Playtime*. Oxford: Success Unlimited.

McMahon, A. and Bolam, R. (1990a) *A Handbook for Primary Schools*. London: Paul Chapman Publishing.

McMahon, A. and Bolam, R (1990b). *A Handbook for Secondary Schools*. London: Paul Chapman Publishing.

Murray, M. and Keane, C. (1998) *The ABC of Bullying*. Dublin: Mercier Press.

Needle, J. (2000) *The Bully*. London: Collins Educational. (This is a play.)

Newman, D.A., Horne, A.M. and Bartolomucci, C.L. (2000) *Bully Busters: A Teacher's Manual for Helping Bullies, Victims and Bystanders*. Champaign ILL: Research Press.

Nicholas, F.M. (1992) *Coping With Conflict: A Resource Book for the Middle School Years*. Wisbech: Learning Development Aids.

Pearce, J. (1989) *Fighting, Teasing and Bullying*. Wellingborough: Thorsons.

Report of the Gulbenkian Foundation. (1995) *Children and Violence*. London: Calouste Gulbenkian Foundation.

Rigby, K. (1996) *Bullying in Schools and What to Do about It*. London: Jessica Kingsley.

Rigby, K. (2002) *New Perspectives on Bullying*. London: Jessica Kingsley.

Robinson, G. and Maines, B. (1997) *Crying for Help: The No Blame Approach to Bullying*. Bristol: Lucky Duck.

Robinson, G., Sleigh, J. and Maines, B. (1995) *No Bullying Starts Today*. Bristol: Lucky Duck.

Romain, T. (1997) *Bullies are a Pain in the Brain*. Minneapolis: Free Spirit.

Ross, C. and Ryan, A. (1990) *Can I Stay in Today, Miss?* Stoke-on-Trent: Trentham Books.

Scherer, M., Gersch, I. and Fry, L. (1992) *Meeting Disruptive Behaviour*. London: Routledge.

Smith, P.K. (ed.) (2003) *Violence in Schools: The Response in Europe*. London: Routledge-Falmer.

Smith, P.K., Morita, Y., Junger-Tas, J., Olweus, D., Catalano, R. and Slee, P. (eds) (1999) *The Nature of School Bullying: A Cross-National Perspective*. London: Routledge.

Smith, P.K. and Sharp, S. (eds) (1998) *School Bullying: Insights and Perspectives*. London: Routledge.

Smith, P.K. and Thompson, D. (1991) *Practical Approaches to Bullying*. London: David Fulton.

Sullivan, K. (2000) *The Anti-Bullying Handbook*. Oxford: Oxford University Press.

Tattum, D. and Lane, D. (eds) (1989) *Bullying in School*. Stoke-on-Trent: Trentham Books.

Thomas, P. (2000) *Stop Picking On Me: A First Look at Bullying*. New York: Barron's Educational Series.

Varma, V.P. (1991) *Truants From Life*. London: David Fulton.

Voors, W. (2000) *The Parent's Book About Bullying*. Center City, MN: Hazelden.

Warren, H. (1984) *Talking About School*. London: London Gay Teenage Group.

Fiction and poetry books for young people

Amos, J. (2001) *Bully*. Bath: Cherrytree Books.

Atwood, M. (1990) *Cat's Eye*. London: Virago Press.

Burley, W.J. (1997) *Wycliffe and the Schoolgirls*. London: Corgi.

Burnard, D. (1996) *Bullysaurus*. London: Hodder Read Alone.

Byrne, J. (1996) *The Bullybuster's Joke Book*. London: Red Fox.

Chambers, A. (1983) *The Present Takers*. London: Red Fox.

Coppard, Y. (1991) *Bully*. London: Red Fox.

Considine, J. (1993) *School Bully*. Dublin: Poolbeg Press.

Cormier, R. (1975) *The Chocolate War*. London: Fontana Lions.

Friel, M. (1993) *Charlie's Story*. Dublin: Poolbeg Press.

Gibbons, A. (1993) *Chicken*. London: Orion Children's Books.

Godden, R. (1991) *The Diddakoi*. London: Pan Macmillan.

Golding, W. (1986) *Lord of the Flies*. London: Macmillan.

Hill, S. (1981) *I'm the King of the Castle*. Harlow: Longman Group.

Hines, B. (1969) *A Kestrel for a Knave*. Harmondsworth: Penguin Books.

Hinton, N. (1988) *Buddy*. Harmondsworth: Penguin Books.

Hinton, N. (1989) *Buddy's Song*. Harmondsworth: Penguin Books.

Hughes, D. (1995) *Bully*. London: Walker Books.

Hughes, T. (1994) *Tom Brown's Schooldays*. Harmondsworth: Penguin Books.

Hunt, R. and Brychta, A. (1995) *The Bully*. Oxford: Oxford University Press.

Kemp, G. (1979) *The Turbulent Term of Tyke Tyler*. Harmondsworth: Penguin Books.
Lee, H. (1974) *To Kill a Mockingbird*. London: Pan Books.
Lee, L. (1959) *Cider with Rosie*. Harmondsworth: Penguin Books.
Leonard, H. (1979) *Home before Night*. Harmondsworth: Penguin Books.
Masters, A. (1997) *Bullies Don't Hurt*. London: Puffin Books.
McGough, R. (1985) *Sky in the Pie*. Harmondsworth: Penguin Books.
Meyer, G. and Meyer, M. (1999) *Just a Bully*. New York: Golden Books.
Needle, J. (1995) *The Bully*. London: Puffin Books.
O'Casey, S. (1963) *I Knock at the Door*. London: Pan Books.
Quirk, Y.C. (1990) *Bully*. London: Bodly Head Children's Books.
Quirk-Walsh, M. (1993) *Searching for a Friend*. Dublin: Attic Press.
Rowling, J.K. (1997) *Harry Potter and the Philosopher's Stone*. London: Bloomsbury.
Simon, F. and Church, C.J. (1999) *Hugo and the Bully Frogs*. London: David and Charles Children's Books.
Stones, R. (1991) *No More Bullying*. Essex: Happy Cat Books.
Townsend, S. (1983) *The Secret Diary of Adrian Mole Aged 13$\frac{3}{4}$*. London: Methuen.
Wilson, W. (1988) *Nine O' Clock Bell: Poems About School*. London: Penguin Books.

INTERNET

Action Alliance for Children. http://www.4children.org
Advisory Centre for Education. http://www.ace-ed.org.uk/bullying
Anti-Bullying Network. http://www.antibully.net/parents/html
Anti-Bullying Research and Resource Centre, Trinity College Dublin. http://www.abc.tcd.ie
BBC Education: Bullying – a Survival Guide. http://www.bbc.co.uk/education/archive/bully/help.html
BBC1 Schools: Bullying. http://www.bbc.co.uk/schools/bullying
Bullying in Schools and What to Do about It (Dr Ken Rigby's pages). http://www.education.unisa.edu.au/bullying
Bullying Online. http://www.bullying.co.uk
Bully Online. http://www.successunlimited.co.uk
Bullystoppers. http://bullystoppers.com/bullying_advice_for_parents.html
Childline. http://www.childline.org.uk
Children's Legal Centre, University of Essex. http://www.essex.ac.uk/clc
Department for Education and Employment. http://www.parents.dfee.gov.uk
Department for Education and Skills: Don't Suffer in Silence. http://www.dfes.gov.uk/bullying/parentsandindex.html
Field Foundation, The. http://www.thefieldfoundation.org
Kidscape. http://www.kidscape.org
Moira Anderson Foundation. http://members.aol.com/sandra7510
National Child Protection Helpline. http://www.nspcc.org.uk
Parent Centre, The. http://www.parentcentre.gov.uk
Parentline Plus. http://www.parentlineplus.org.uk
Scottish Anti-Bullying Network. http://www.antibullying.net
Scottish Council for Research in Education. http://www.scre.ac.uk
Scottish Executive. Let's Stop Bullying: Advice for Parents and Families. http://www.scotland.gov.uk/library2/doc04/lsbp-00.html
Suzy Lamplugh Trust. http://www.suzylamplugh.org
Teacherline. http://www.teacherline.org.uk
UK Department for Education and Employment (DfEE). http:dfee.gov.uk/bullying/pages/home.html
VISYON. http://www.visyon.org.uk
Young Minds. http://www.youngminds.org.uk
Youth 2 Youth. http://www.youth2youth.co.uk

RESOURCE PACKS AND VIDEOS FOR SCHOOLS AND PARENTS

Policy and awareness-raising packs

Besag, V. (1992) *We Don't Have Bullies Here!* 57 Manor House Road, Jesmond, Newcastle-upon-Tyne, NE2 2LY.

Browne, K. (1995) *Bully Off: Towards a Whole New Ball Game of Relationships in Schools.* First and Best in Education Ltd.

Foundation for Peace Studies, Aotearoa / New Zealand (1994) *Cool Schools Mediation Programme.* Auckland: Foundation for Peace Studies.

Robinson, G., Sleigh, J. and Maines, B. (1995) *No Bullying Starts Today: An Awareness Raising Pack.* Bristol: Lucky Duck.

Scottish Consultative Council on the Curriculum (1992) *Speak Up – An Anti-Bullying Resource Pack.* Dundee: SCCC.

Scottish Council for Research in Education (1993) *Supporting Schools Against Bullying.* Edinburgh: SCRE.

Slee, P. (1997) *The P.E.A.C.E. Pack: Reducing Bullying in our Schools.* Adelaide: School of Education, Flinders University.

Video packs

Brown, T. (1993) *Broken Toy.* Bristol: Lucky Duck.

Brown, T., Robinson, G. and Maines, B. (1998) *But Names Will Never Hurt Me.* Bristol: Lucky Duck.

Department of Education and Employment (2000) *Don't Suffer in Silence: An Anti-Bullying Pack for Schools.* London: HMSO.

Robinson, G. and Maines, B. (1992) *Stamp Out Bullying.* Bristol: Lucky Duck.

Video films

Hands on Bullying. (1998) Tony Jewes Productions.

The Trouble with Tom. (1991) Central Independent Television Productions.

Welcome to the Dollhouse. (1995) Produced by Donna Bascom and Todd Solandz. (Feature-length movie: over 15s).

BULLYING IN THE WORKPLACE: REFERENCES FOR SCHOOL STAFF AND OTHERS

Books

Adams, A. and Crawford, N. (1992) *Bullying at Work.* London: Virago Press.

Clifton, J. and Serdar, H. (2000) *Bully Off: Recognising and Tackling Workplace Bullying.* Dorset: Russell House.

Einarsen, S., Hoel, H., Zapf, D. and Cooper, C.L. (2003) *Bullying and Emotional Abuse in the Workplace. International Perspectives in Research and Practise.* London: Taylor & Francis.

Evans, P. (1996) *The Verbally Abusive Relationship: How to Recognise it and How to Respond.* London: Adams.

Field, T. (1996) *Bully in Sight: How to Predict, Resist, Challenge and Combat Workplace Bullying.* Oxford: Success Unlimited.

Kelly, J. (1999) *Bully Proof: Handling Harassment at Work.* London: Aurora Books.

Kinchin, D. (1998) *Post-Traumatic Stress Disorder: The Invisible Injury.* Oxford: Success Unlimited.

Namie, G. and Namie, R. (2000) *The Bully at Work.* Naperville, ILL: Sourcebooks.

Randall, P. (1997) *Adult Bullying: Perpetrators and Victims.* London: Routledge.

Ryan, K.D. and Oestreich, D.K. (1988) *Driving Fear out of the Workplace.* San Fransisco: Jossey Bass.

Sapolsky, R.M. (1998) *Why Zebras Don't Get Ulcers: An Updated Guide to Stress, Stress-Related Diseases and Coping*. New York: Freeman.
Solomon, M. (1990) *Working with Difficult People*. London: Prentice Hall.

Journal articles and reports

Brooks-Gordon, B. (1999) 'Sexual harassment in the workplace', *Journal of Occupational and Organisational Psychology*, 72 (1): 117–19.
Di Martino, V., Hoel, H. and Cooper, C.L. (2003) 'Preventing violence and harassment in the workplace', report for the European Foundation for the Improvement of Living and Working Conditions.
Einarsen, S. (1999) 'The nature and causes of bullying at work', *International Journal of Manpower*, 20, 16–27.
Hoel, H., Cooper, C.L. and Faragher, B. (2001) 'The experience of bullying in Great Britain: the impact of organisation status', *European Journal of Work and Organisational Psychology*, 16: 443–66.
Leymann, H. (1996) 'The content and development of mobbing at work', *European Journal of Work and Organisational Psychology*, 5 (2): 251–75.
O'Moore, A.M., Seigne, E., McGuire, L. and Smith, M. (1998) 'Victims of workplace bullying in Ireland', *Irish Journal of Psychology*, 19 (2–3): 345–57.
O'Moore, A.M., Lynch, J. and Nic Daeid, N. (2003) 'The rates and relative risks of workplace bullying in Ireland, a country of high economic growth', *International Journal of Management and Decision Making*, 4 (1): 82–95.
Raynor, C. and Hoel, H. (1997) 'A summary review of literature relating to workplace bullying' *Journal of Community and Applied Social Psychology*, 1: 181–91.
Sheehan, M. and Barker, M. (1998) 'Bullying at work: an international perspective', *Journal of Occupational Health and Safety*, 14 (6): 587–92.
Zapf, D., Knorz, C. and Kulla, M. (1996) 'On the relationship between mobbing factors, job content, social work environment and health outcomes', *European Journal of Work and Organisational Psychology*, 5 (2): 215–37.

Index